By Sir Arthur Quiller-Couch

On the Art of Writing
On the Art of Reading
Adventures in Criticism
Charles Dickens and Other Victorians
Studies in Literature
Studies in Literature, 2nd Series
Studies in Literature, 3rd Series

Studies in Literature

Third Series

Studies in Literature

Third Series

By

Sir Arthur Quiller-Couch, M.A.

Fellow of Jesus College
King Edward VII Professor of English Literature
in the University of Cambridge

New York: G. P. Putnam's Sons
Cambridge, England: University Press
1930

STUDIES IN LITERATURE

THIRD SERIES

PREFACE

MOST of the following discourses were given to my pupils in the New Arts Schools at Cambridge. In one of them—a practical talk *On Reading for the English Tripos* here—I have made bold to use or repeat some paragraphs from *A Lecture on Lectures* published in 1927 by The Hogarth Press. The lecture on *Shakespeare's Comedies* inaugurating a week's session on Shakespeare at Oxford had, of necessity, to be general in outline; and might perhaps be better entitled *The Quiddity of a Shakespeare Comedy*. The pages on Longinus profess no more than to be a note, re-introducing that fine but neglected critic to the attention of students in English. The serious editions of him, of Dionysius and of Demetrius, by the late Dr. W. Rhys Roberts, with his translations and commentaries, have long seemed to me a κτῆμα for all practitioners of style in writing.

The paper on Coventry Patmore, reprinted from the *Monthly Review* (now unhappily defunct), was originally written as a critique of his *Biography,* published so long ago as 1900 by Mr. Basil Champneys. I leave it as it stood; but now recognise that certain personal and irrelevant claims for him, made about that time by worshippers (and especially by co-religionists who seemed to me to confuse good poetry with their concept of what makes for salvation), occupied much of the attention that had better have been employed in praising.

Preface

The two "lectures" *On the New Reading Public* were never spoken, but have been condensed and converted into lecture form out of some six articles I was invited to contribute to *John O' London's Weekly.*

The last two items were not lectures at all, but addresses; the one given at Hampstead as a brief prelude to dedicating the home of John Keats; the other a speech at Edinburgh proposing a toast to the immortal memory of Scott.

Q.

November, 1929

CONTENTS

	PAGE
PREFACE	V
THE ENGLISH ELEGY (I)	3
THE ENGLISH ELEGY (II)	25
THE JOURNALS OF DOROTHY WORDSWORTH (I)	54
DOROTHY WORDSWORTH (II)	76
SHAKESPEARE'S COMEDIES	101
COVENTRY PATMORE	122
A NOTE ON LONGINUS	143
ON READING FOR THE ENGLISH TRIPOS	162
ON "THE NEW READING PUBLIC" (I)	182
ON "THE NEW READING PUBLIC" (II)	198
W. S. GILBERT	216
OPENING OF KEATS HOUSE, HAMPSTEAD	241
THE MEMORY OF SIR WALTER SCOTT	248
INDEX	259

STUDIES IN LITERATURE

THE ENGLISH ELEGY (I)

I

EVERYONE in this room, I suppose, remembers Dr. Johnson's notorious criticism of *Lycidas;* and almost everyone, I hope, to condemn it.

One of the poems on which much praise has been bestowed is *Lycidas;* of which the diction is harsh, the rhymes uncertain, and the numbers unpleasing.

He goes on:

What beauty there is, we must therefore seek in the sentiments and images. It is not to be considered as the effusion of real passion: for passion runs not after remote allusions and obscure opinions. Passion plucks no berries from the myrtle and ivy, nor calls upon Arethuse and Mincius, nor tells of rough satyrs and fauns with cloven hoof. Where there is leisure for fiction there is little grief.

Now there is this eminent merit of usefulness in Johnson, that, right or wrong, he always speaks definitely, so that you always know where you are with him: a merit which Mr. Robert Bridges at once claims for himself and justifies in his famous *Essay on Keats.* "If," says he, "my criticism should seem sometimes harsh, that is, I believe, due to its being given in plain terms; a method which I prefer, because by obliging the

3

writer to say definitely what he means it makes his mistakes easy to point out, and in this way the true business of criticism is advanced."

Well, in the passage I have quoted from his "Life" of Milton, Johnson, by saying definitely what he means, definitely protrudes two fallacies: and I take them as our text to-day, Gentlemen, not for any tedious renewed examination (Heaven forbid!) of Johnson's injustice to Milton, but as points of disagreement and departure from which to open some reflections on the English Elegy, its tradition, what our classics aimed at in practising it, how perchance (since we are all born to lament sooner or later, in words or silence) our sons may lament us.

II

Now the first of Johnson's fallacies exposes itself in the words "it is not to be considered as the effusion of real passion." Who said "passion"?

We shall come to the circumstance of *Lycidas*—to discuss also its form and intent—by and by. Here let us note that the word "passion" may bear for us either one of two different meanings, as Dr. Johnson (that great lexicographer) perfectly well knew. It may mean simply suffering, as when we speak of Christ's death and "passion," though even so, maybe, with some sense of the word's secondary meaning as we recall—consciously or not—His agony in the Garden. For the word's secondary meaning slides passive into active: we use it of love, desire, anger—"the red rose breathes of passion," "Lear's passionate hate," "passionate tears": and obviously what Johnson wishes us to think of is *this* passion—the passion which, reacting immediately and violently upon the stroke of sorrow, drives us (as the saying is) beyond ourselves.

Johnson had no children, to die before him. Had such a stroke befallen him, he would have known—as an imaginative man might have guessed—something of that awful void with which, since it takes away hope, even the desolation of an orphan will not compare. Under such extremity of bereavement as that, or as the snatching by death of one of two utter lovers, bridegroom or bride, grief without hope plucks, indeed, no berries from the myrtle and ivy. But neither does it write Elegies at all. It is dumb: even tears come hardly and through agony of relief. "I tell you," says Mrs. Browning, in a most solemn sonnet:

I tell you, hopeless grief is passionless;
  That only men incredulous of despair,
  Half-taught in anguish, through the midnight **air**
Beat upward to God's throne in loud access
Of shrieking and reproach. Full desertness
  In souls as countries lieth silent—bare
  Under the blanching, vertical eye-glare
Of the absolute Heavens.

                  Deep-hearted man, express
Grief for thy dead in silence like to death—
  Most like a monumental statue set
  In everlasting watch and moveless woe,
Till itself crumble to the dust beneath.
  Touch it; the marble eyelids are not wet:
  If it could weep, it could arise and go.

So we have grief most desperate interpreted for us in Ugolino's *Io non piangeva;* symbolised for us in Niobe, not "all tears" but with breasts frozen to stone. If,

however, there be ever so little of revolt, which spells
some indignation, some defiance, grief will vent itself in
tears, outcries, curses, challenges to God—"Why should
this be? What has love done to deserve this cruelty?
Is it just to punish us so—us, that have walked humbly
and been innocently happy? Is it wrong in God's eyes
to have been thus happy in those nests of family and
friendship we have built for ourselves?"

But these are accusations, outcries. And these outcries are not Elegy. As an old writer in *The Quarterly
Review* wisely commented on the very passage of Johnson's we are considering—

There is no universal language of grief. It takes its complexion from the country, the age, the individual. In its
paroxysms no man thinks of writing verses of any kind. We
exclaim, as King David does, "My son! My son!" When the
paroxysm is past, every man will write such verses (if he
write them at all) as the ordinary turn of his mind dictates.

That again is true enough in its way. As Johnson,
if we talk of immediate grief, is right in telling us that
passion plucks no berries from the myrtle and ivy, nor
calls upon Arethusa and Mincius, equally, and just so
far, is our *Quarterly* reviewer right in telling us that in
paroxysms of grief no man thinks of writing verses of
any kind.

III

But there, I suggest to you, their wisdom ends; or their
insight, at any rate, into the conditions and meaning of
Elegiac verse. Men *do* write Elegies in Country Church-
yards, as men wrote them on Sicilian slopes, and their
melodious commonplaces on the theme of death have had
power to move the moveable generations of men.

For who, to dumb Forgetfulness a prey,
   This pleasing anxious being e'er resign'd,
Left the warm precincts of the cheerful day,
   Nor cast one longing ling'ring look behind?

On some fond breast the parting soul relies,
   Some pious drops the closing eye requires,
E'en from the tomb the voice of Nature cries,
   E'en in our ashes live their wonted fires.

There is high emotion here, not passion: such high and solemn emotion as all sensitive men must feel who reflect upon Death—most universal of commonplaces. "Laodameia died, Helen died . . ." "When thou must home to shades of underground . . ." "Consider that great day when we shall all of us be contemporaries . . ." "Pulvis et umbra . . ." "In a little dust quiescent . . ." "Then shall the dust return to the earth as it was; and the spirit shall return unto God which gave it . . ." These phrases haunt us—you may multiply them for yourselves by the hundred—but they are not words of passion. Feelings of awe proper to us in Westminster Abbey have been expressed well enough by Francis Beaumont:

Mortality, behold, and fear,
What a change of flesh is here! . . .
Here the bones of birth have cried
"Though gods they were, as men they died":
Here are sands, ignoble things,
Dropt from the ruin'd sides of kings. . . .

—expressed well enough, too, by Addison, and again by Washington Irving. Gray takes us from the Abbey to a Country Churchyard, and there, amid the graves of the cottage poor, universalises the theme. His is a *general*

Elegy, and wrung from Johnson (who loved generalisa-
tion, but disliked Gray in particular) the famous admission that "it abounds with images which find a mirror
in every mind, and with sentiments to which every heart
returns an echo." It is superbly done, and probably, as
a general Elegy and as a whole, will never be beaten,
although (as Mrs. Meynell once pointed out) in separate
lines it falls to the besetting disaster of the general
commonplace, which is commonplaceness.

> Full many a flower is born to blush unseen,
> And waste its sweetness on the desert air.

But Shakespeare before this had written,

> The summer's flower is to the summer sweet,
> Though to itself it only live and die, . . .

—Still, a noble poem: but monumental, not passionate.
Shakespeare, not writing *Elegy*, swoops down on such
levelling of greatness, in a passion, tooth and claw. Hear
doomed Cleopatra, "lass unparallel'd," rushing into the
secret house of death amid the outcries of her hand-
maids.

<pre>
                          the odds is gone,
                And there is nothing left remarkable
                Beneath the visiting moon.
Charmian.   O, quietness, lady!
Iras.   She's dead too, our Sovereign.
Charmian.   Lady!
Iras.   Madam!
Charmian.   O madam, madam, madam!
Iras.   Royal Egypt!
                Empress!
Charmian.   Peace, peace, Iras!
</pre>

Cleopatra. No more, but e'en a woman, and commanded
By such poor passion as the maid that milks
And does the meanest chares. It were for me
To throw my sceptre at the injurious gods;
To tell them that this world did equal theirs
Till they had stolen our jewel.

Or hear Donne on the fragments of Jesabel.

The dust of great persons' graves is speechless too: it says nothing, it distinguishes nothing. . . . So is the death of Jesabel (Jesabel was a Queen) expressed. They shall not say "This is Jesabel"; not only not wonder that it is, nor pity that it should be, but they shall not say, they shall not know, This is Jesabel.

IV

I have brought you thus far, Gentlemen, of purpose to a point where we may begin to philosophise the Elegy as a poetic form. We may not rule out immediate passion: for, to begin with, its outcries have often in drama (though seldom in Elegy) reached nobility. Nor do I forget that though the first effect of grief is commonly a petrifying stupor, often (as I have observed in men and women during the late War) it lifts to a strange exaltation of mind, causing the bereaved to talk and even to walk as gods, elevated in a great calm above common daily hopes, anxieties, fears, since they were for *his* sake and with him have been taken away at a stroke. Sorrow is their throne, and "let kings come bow to it."

Most of us have observed this strange calm of woe in others; some of us have felt it: and it does not write Elegies. But as few men are without a religion of their own, or a philosophy, or at least a habit of fortitude

enabling them (as the phrase is) to carry on, so upon—
I call that not recovery, for the object is irrecoverable
and life can never again be what it was—but upon
acceptance there supervenes a pathetic desire to perpetuate, even to decorate our dead : and here comes in the
Elegy's true function.

Idle to tell us, as Sir Thomas Browne does, that we
cannot perpetuate, that "Diaturnity is a dream and folly
of expectation!" If you wish a sermon on that text with
a wealth of instances, you may find it in his *Urn-Burial;*
with a wealth of wise saws, too.—"But the iniquity of
oblivion blindly scattereth her poppy." "There is nothing strictly immortal, but immortality!" True. But
the desire of it is perennial in man and will only be
destroyed with the last of our race, himself "still clutch-
ing the inviolable shade." And this desire, if you
examine it, has its very root in our own realised transience—as Anteros is of one womb with Eros.

> Forsooth the present we must give
>   To that which cannot pass away;
> All beauteous things for which we live
>   By laws of time and space decay.
> But O, the very reason why
> We clasp them, is because they die!

After all, any great Elegy solves this question of per-
petuating *ambulando*. Edward King of Christ's College
died close on three hundred years ago, yet will survive
through *Lycidas* while English Literature lasts—which
we all piously hope will be a long time.

As for *decorating* our dead—well, I shall presently
discuss that instinct of ours : but for the moment I
merely put it to you that the poet who builds a shrine of

verse to a dead friend or a dead mistress, elaborating it
with all offerings his art can bring—

With the wreath'd trellis of a working brain

—obeys a like impulse with that which rears a Taj
Mahal, and heaps flowers at the base of the Whitehall
Cenotaph. *Manibus date lilia plenis.*

V

To be sure, if we speak only of *Lycidas,* we may yield
a point further to Johnson. What I have just been saying does not apply to *Lycidas* quite as it applies (say) to
In Memoriam.

Arthur Henry Hallam died in 1833: Tennyson's
monody upon him did not appear until 1850. The interval of seventeen years not only gave the mourner ample
time to reconsider his first passion of grief and, recon-
sidering, to universalise it, to philosophise it, to adorn it
carefully, monumentally, and so make of it a poem for
any man who has ever lost a friend. The interval, in a
way, convinces of itself. We reckon that long silence of
brooding, and "Here," we say, "is no faggot of grief
quick to blaze, soon spent up the chimney, but a log
rather that—to borrow a phrase of Landor's—leans back
upon the hearth with the slow fire in its core."

Now Edward King, aged twenty-five only, Fellow and
Tutor of Christ's College, who had been an undergraduate with Milton, though junior—a youth of golden
opinions—was drowned in shipwreck off the Welsh
coast on August 10th, 1637. "The news," says Masson,
"caused a profound sensation among all King's friends.

"As it was the time of the University vacation, when

his college-fellows were scattered, it must have reached them separately, and some of them circuitously . . ."

When the Cambridge colleges reassembled in October . . . the melancholy death of poor King of Christ's was one of the first subjects of talk.

It was proposed by somebody, or it suggested itself to more than one at once, that a volume of Memorial Verse should be prepared in his honour and published from the University Press.

Milton, who had left Cambridge five years before and was now rusticating in his father's house at Horton in Buckinghamshire, would naturally be solicited for a contribution: and so *Lycidas* came to be written in November 1637 and to find its way, signed "J.M.," into a collection of tributes from some thirty others, published in 1638 and entitled "*Justa Edouardo King naufrago ab amicis moerentibus, amoris et μνείας χάριν*" (Rites to Edward King, drowned in shipwreck, in love and remembrance by his sorrowing friends).

This much is historical of course: but I cannot find evidence that King and Milton had been close bosom friends as Milton and Charles Diodati were, or as Tennyson and Hallam, unless we express their uttermost meaning from the exquisite lines:

For we were nurst upon the self-same hill,
Fed the same flock, by fountain, shade and rill.
    Together both, ere the high Lawns appear'd
Under the opening eye-lids of the morn,
We drove a-field, and both together heard
What time the Gray-fly winds her sultry horn,
Batt'ning our flocks with the fresh dews of night,
Oft till the Star that rose, at Ev'ning, bright
Towards Heav'ns descent had slop'd his westering wheel.

Tush! says Johnson. "We know that they never drove a-field, and that they had no flocks to batten"—which is, ultimately, rubbish and (if I may put it so) just the old man's way, now and then, when there was no admonitory voice to warn *"Samuel!—Samuel!"* But immediately and for his unholy purpose he had this much of right.

Exquisite though they are, the lines have not that convincing note of personal loss which tolls through Cowley's Elegy upon another Cambridge man, William Hervey—

Say, for you saw us, ye immortal lights,
How oft unwearied have we spent the nights,
Till the Ledaean stars, so famed for love,
    Wonder'd at us from above!

We spent them not in toys, in lusts, or wine;
    But search of deep Philosophy,
    Wit, Eloquence, and Poetry—
Arts which I loved, for they, my Friend, were Thine.

Ye fields of Cambridge, our dear Cambridge, say
Have ye not seen us walking every day;
Was there a tree about which did not know
    The love betwixt us two?

Henceforth, ye gentle trees, for ever fade;
    Or your sad branches thicker join
    And into darksome shades combine,
Dark as the grave wherein my friend is laid!

VI

So much we may conclude; as also that *Lycidas,* for all its beauties, betrays some haste in its structural design.

But Johnson is wrong, utterly wrong, when he goes on to object that "Among the flocks and copses and flowers appear the heathen deities, Love and Phoebus, Neptune and Aeolus, with a long train of mythological imagery, such as a College easily supplies."

Worse, he was sinning against his own knowledge. For no one knew better than Johnson that Milton, so far from innovating with a peculiar fault, was strictly following a tradition of Elegy—even English Elegy— even a tradition which lasted to Johnson's own day, as it has survived him.

It does not astonish me that Johnson (who, let me remind you, went straight back to Juvenal for his Satires, *London* and *The Vanity of Human Wishes*—who again, on being asked to compose an English epitaph upon Goldsmith, roundly told Sir Joshua Reynolds, bearer of the request, that "he would never consent to disgrace the walls of Westminster Abbey with an English inscription")—I say it does not astonish me that Johnson, being Johnson, wrote the above: for Johnson in argument, as physically, was short-sighted, occupied with immediate triumph; careless that to persuade, though it cost more patience, is finally more effective than to stun. Moreover, before Johnson's time there had crept in a notion among critics and religious poets that the gods of Greece and Rome were *démodés,* or at any rate ought to be, and that serious Christian poets ought somehow to expel them. Cowley, whom I quoted to you just now, puts it thus in his lines on the death of Crashaw—

> Still the old heathen gods in numbers dwell,
> The heavenliest thing on earth still keeps up hell.
> Nor have we yet quite purged the Christian land;
> Still idols here, like calves at Bethel, stand.

And though Pan's death long since all oracles broke,
Yet still in rhyme the fiend Apollo spoke:
Nay, with the worst of heathen dotage we
(Vain men!) the monster woman deify;
Find stars, and tie our fates there in a face,
And Paradise in them, by whom we lost it, place.
What different faults corrupt our muses thus!
Wanton as girls, as old wives fabulous!

In prose he asks "Are the obsolete threadbare tales of Thebes and Troy half so stored with great heroical and supernatural actions as the wars of Joshua and the Judges, of David and divers others?"

Well, one answer to that is, the flat one, "Yes, they are: and not only half so stored, but a hundred times more so." To such theorists we might add the demand, "Produce your poem on the massacre of Ai, the fall of Jericho; or say where you have in practice preferred to the story of Harmodius and Aristogeiton that of the murder of Eglon, a very fat man, by Ehud, who made himself a dagger." For my part, as the student of what poets write, I remark that while they go on inveterately dreaming of obsolete threadbare Helen and Iseult, of Phoebus Apollo and his sister Dian, of the fields of Enna and the lists of Camelot, they incline to let the great Biblical characters speak for themselves. Why, I quoted just now Cowley's own Elegy upon William Hervey—Cowley at his most passionate. What compelled him, holding his opinion, to insert Castor and Pollux into his lament for William Hervey?—

Till the Ledaean stars, so famed for love,
Wonder'd at us from above!

VII

Our answer is that Cowley wrote in this "classical" fashion, as Milton had written in it, because the Elegiac tradition *compelled* them, as it had compelled almost all their predecessors in French, Italian and English Elegy, and may be said to dominate the Elegy to quite recent times and to hold its own even yet.

We have now to examine this tradition and ask how it was derived.

The Greeks, from Homer down, combined a very lively, though catholic, sense of religion, with a very poignant sense of death; of the end of life, but also of the happy ones, the gods, glorified beings in man's image, who preside over his life while it lasts, themselves immortal.

"Give this stranger, too, the cup," says Peisistratus in the *Odyssey,* "since he too, methinks, must pray to the immortals. All men have need of gods."

But the Greeks of what we roughly call the "best period" had no use for Elegy. If they had, they would have discovered it. Their personal mourning was austere, almost always brief, albeit often perfect within its brevity. They spoke in monumental inscriptions, and this was how they spoke:

The daughters of Samos often wish Crethis back, the chatterbox, who knew pretty games, sweetest of workmates, ever talking: but she has shut her eyes here in the dream we must all dream.

Or

The sea is the sea. Why chide the Cyclades or the race by Hellè or off the Needles?—since I escaped them to drown by

Scarphè, in harbour. Pray who will for a fair wind home.
The sea knows the sea's way: and so do I, Aristagoras, buried
here.

Or

   Rest beneath the poplars here, O traveller, and drink beside
our spring; so depart, but however far thou farest, remember
the fountain that Simus builds by the side of Gallus his dead
boy.

Or take about the earliest and most famous of these
composers of epitaphs, Simonides (B.C. 556–467), a
native of Ceos who spent a great part of his life in
Athens: and take his most famous epigram of all, of
two lines only, on the Spartans who died defending
Thermopylae—

> Ὦ ξεῖν', ἀγγέλλειν Λακεδαιμονίοις, ὅτι τῇδε
> κείμεθα, τοῖς κείνων ῥήμασι πειθόμενοι.

—that is, translating the untranslateable,

> Tell them in Lacedaemon, passer by,
> We kept the Spartan code, and here we lie.

—always, you see, the like brevity, the like economy of
emotion. To match that in English you must go to stray
lines such as Macbeth's

> She should have died hereafter:

or Horatio's

> Good night, sweet prince,
> And flights of angels sing thee to thy rest!

Or for inscriptions, complete and compact, to Andrew Marvell's *Epitaph on a Lady:*

> Modest as morn, as mid-day bright,
> Gentle as evening, cool as night:
> —'Tis true: but all too weakly said,
> 'Twas more significant, she's dead—

or to the distich on Sir Albert Morton's widow:

> He first deceased; she for a little tried
> To live without him, liked it not, and died.

But the Elegy as a poetic form does not derive from the Epitaph. Historically it derives from the Pastoral, and can scarcely be separated from it in our studies. The Pastoral has fallen out of fashion in these days and into the easy contempt of the critics—to my mind, the undeserved contempt. It earned at any rate a very respectable livelihood in its time. I do not, however, propose to discuss the Pastoral with you to-day apart from the Elegy's connection with it.

Historically, then, the Elegy is a *form* of that Pastoral verse which the Greek poets of Sicily—Theocritus, Bion, Moschus—elevated (very likely from the folk-song of actual shepherds) into a species of artistic poetry in and about the first half of the 3rd century B.C. Theocritus, a Syracusan exiled (probably by his own ambition) into the city and court life of Alexandria, remembered and regretted the fields of his home, re-nowned then as today for their amazing wealth of flowers, their encircling hills, with Etna and the blue sea, and turned into poetry the verse contests in which the shepherds of that island traditionally engaged—somewhat we may say as Burns transformed the rude songs of Ayrshire into the lyrics that we know. Let us remind ourselves that contest, competition, was part and an essential part of the Greek spirit in "music" as well as "gymnastic." To quote Sir Edmund Chambers—

Upon Theocritus . . . those bucolic rhythms, remembered so well from his childhood, had all the fascination which the simple exercises over the complex, a fascination wrought out of contrast and reminiscence. He wove them into poems of a delicate artificiality, preserving the main outlines of the actual life from which they sprang, but emphasizing all the comely elements therein, and rendering them with a keener sense of natural beauty, a more subtle music of the Doric speech, than ever yet glorified any oaten pipe at any festival of Artemis. Certain traditional forms Theocritus fixed upon the pastoral for all time; the singing match for some rustic wager, a soft white lamb, a carven drinking bowl of beechwood or of maple; the bout of rude bantering between two rival swains; the sad lament of a lover for unrequited or deceived love; the dirge of his fellows around the tomb of some dead shepherd, Daphnis or another, who in his time had himself well known to build the lofty rhyme among them. These forms, taken no doubt from actual memories of Himera or Syracuse, Theocritus bequeathed to his successors in the ways of the pastoral muse, and with them that absorption in the amorous theme, which is after all from beginning to end the dominant note of his lyric.

Now of these Idylls, as they are called, one of the most characteristic was the Elegy or lament. The very first, if not most famous, in Theocritus contains such a lament on the shepherd Daphnis, a Sicilian hero-shepherd to whom legend ascribed the invention of bucolic poetry. Whether this Daphnis was an actual person or not we need not pause to enquire, or to examine the

accounts of Aelian and Athenaeus as to the various ways
in which he met his death, the most poetical of which is
that he fell a victim to the Phrygian king Lityerses, who
compelled all strangers to vie with him in reaping his
corn and then killed them when they were defeated: as
Matthew Arnold sings in *Thyrsis*—

Thou hearest the immortal chants of old!
   Putting his sickle to the perilous grain
     In the hot cornfield of the Phrygian king,
   For thee the Lityerses-song again
     Young Daphnis with his silver voice doth sing;
      Sings his Sicilian fold,
His sheep, his hapless love, his blinded eyes—
   And how a call celestial round him rang,
   And heavenward from the fountain-brink he sprang,
And all the marvel of the golden skies.

Nor again need we trouble ourselves here with the
theory (for which you may study Sir James Frazer's
Golden Bough) that this Daphnis was the personification
of the corn spirit, its death in harvest and resurrection
in the Spring; nor yet again enquire too curiously how
far the chant was bound up with the belief that song
could call the dead back from Hades, as—

   —when Sicilian shepherds lost a mate,
     Some good survivor with his flute would go,
   Piping a ditty sad for Bion's fate;
     And cross the unpermitted ferry's flow,
      And relax Pluto's brow,
   And make leap up with joy the beauteous head
     Of Proserpine, among whose crownèd hair
     Are flowers first open'd on Sicilian air,
   And flute his friend, like Orpheus, from the dead.

O easy access to the hearer's grace
  When Dorian shepherds sang to Proserpine!
    For she herself had trod Sicilian fields,
  She knew the Dorian water's gush divine,
    She knew each lily white which Enna yields,
      Each rose with blushing face;
  She loved the Dorian pipe, the Dorian strain.
    But ah, of our poor Thames she never heard!
    Her foot the Cumnor cowslips never stirr'd;
  And we should tease her with our plaint in vain!

It is enough for us that Thyrsis laments the shepherd
Daphnis, the sweet singer, "a man by the nymphs beloved, and the Muses called him friend," with a descant—

Lift, lift our Muses again, the dirge of the pastures!

Moschus follows Theocritus in his lovely lament for
Bion:

Lament, lament, O woodlands and sweet Dorian water: ye
rivers, too, lament Bion our darling! Orchards and groves,
make mourn: flowers, breathe your sighs, all with petals
dishevelled. Rose, anemone, flower-de-luce—our lovely Bion
is dead, our maker of music,—*Sing woe, sing woe, ye Muses
of Sicily!*

If you read these laments for Daphnis and for Bion
carefully you will find the whole secret of the English
Elegy to be taken from Sicily. Virgil stole it for Italy
and in his lovely fifth Eclogue translates Daphnis from
the sheepcotes to the stars and sets him on the threshold
of heaven:

Candidus insuetum miratur limen Olympi
Sub pedibusque videt nubes et sidera Daphnis—

—even as Rossetti figured The Blessed Damozel, leaning over the bar of Heaven and looking down, far down, into

> The void, as low as where this earth
> Spins like a fretful midge.

So from the pattern of Virgil our earlier Elegists derive their form. The pattern is constant. "Lament, ye shepherds and shepherdesses, ye Muses also. Our flocks feed not, our ewes breed not, Apollo is concerned: the mountains make moan and the little hills, since So-and-so is dead." So it persists for us over three centuries of our poesy: and I shall ask you, after listening to some stanzas of Spenser, to note how true feeling can transfigure a formal mode of verse; how the breast, so to speak, can shine through the corselet while the corselet dignifies the breast. The stanzas are from *Daphnaida,* "an Elegie upon the death of the noble and vertuous Douglas Howard, Daughter and heire of Henry, Lord Howard, Viscount Byndon, and wife of Arthure Gorges Esquire." (Doctor Johnson, in fractious mood, might object that the daughter of Lord Howard was not called Daphne and never kept sheep.)

> How happie was I, when I saw her leade
> The Shepheards daughters dauncing in a rownd?
> How trimly would she trace and softly tread
> The tender grasse with rosie garland crownd?
> And when she list aduance her heaunly voyce,
> Both Nimphs and Muses nigh she made astownd
> And flocks and shepheards caus̀ed to rejoyce.
>
> But now ye shepheard lasses, who shall lead
> Your wandring troupes, or sing your virelayes?

Or who shall dight your bowres sith she is dead
That was the Lady of your holy dayes?
Let now your blisse be turnèd into bale,
And into plaints conuert your joyous playes,
And with the same fill every hill and dale . . .

For I will walke this wandring pilgrimage
Throughout the world from one to other end,
And in affliction waste my bitter age.
My bread shall be the anguish of my mind . . .

Ne sleepe (the harbenger of wearie wights)
Shall ever lodge upon mine ey-lids more:
Ne shall with rest refresh my fainting spright,
Nor failing force to former strength restore:
But I will wake and sorrow all the night
With *Philomene,* my fortune to deplore,
With *Philomene,* the partner of my plight.

And euer as I see the starres to fall,
And under ground to goe, to giue them light
Which dwell in darkness, I to minde will call
How my faire Starre (that shinde on me so bright)
Fell sodainly, and faded under ground;
Since whose departure day is turned to night,
And night without a Venus starre is found . . .

And she my love that was, my Saint that is,
When she beholds from her celestiall throne,
(In which she joyeth in eternall blisse)
My bitter penance, will my case bemone,
And pitie me that living thus doo die:
For heavenly spirits have compassion
On mortall men, and rue their miserie.

So when I have with sorrowe satisfide
Th' importune fates, which vengeance on me seeke,

And th' Heauns with long languor pacifide,
She, for pure pitie of my sufferance meeke,
Will send for me; for which I daylie long,
And will till then my painfull penance eeke:
Weep, Shepheard, weep to make my under song!

THE ENGLISH ELEGY (II)

I

WE saw Gentlemen, in our previous Lecture that the Elegy, derived ultimately from Theocritus through Virgil, came into our literature as an exotic; as indeed it had come into the literatures of Italy and France long before Spenser took it in hand. As Sir Edmund Chambers says, we cannot claim of it as we can claim of the contemporary romantic drama with a proper pride, that we are dealing with an essentially national growth. The drama of the Elizabethans sprang up in Thames-side theatres, and took its unmistakable character as it was fostered by the demands and applause of its audiences, which included the fashionable courtier with the apprentice in the cheap gallery. But the beginnings of our earlier literature, both in prose and poetry (if we exclude the Ballads), were essentially aristocratic, taking their impulse from classical models and encouraged, for any commercial value they possessed, by the patronage of kings and noblemen: and we have discussed together before now the processes through which our authors have come to appeal to the large public of today.

But the innovation of our forefathers, first of all by daring to write in the vernacular, and again by daring to use native idioms and rhythms, had at first to be cautious, as at any time they might be pushed on to the defensive by supercilious scholars. Examine the correspondence between Spenser and Gabriel Harvey and you will see how nearly the *Faerie Queene* escaped being attempted in hexameters.

But though he took the Eclogue as an exotic, Spenser could command a native impulse to help him in transferring the scenery of Sicily and Etruria to that of his own country, the whisper in the pine-tops to the large breezes blowing over our sheep-downs. In his time city life (the noise and pressure of London) was a new and concentrated and hectic thing; and a quiet mind reverted to the previous century when England was most characteristically a land of sheep-farms and the poetic mind could retire upon its memories as, in the century to follow, it retired to gardens and planted orchards from the occupations of civil warfare, noise of cannon and pulpit strife. As Dryden afterwards said, in dedicating his translation of *The Pastorals of Virgil* to Lord Clifford, after a comparison of Theocritus and Virgil:

Our own nation has produced a third poet in this kind, not inferior to the two former. For the *Shepherd's Calendar* of Spenser is not to be matched in any modern language: not even by Tasso's *Aminta,* which infinitely transcends Guarini's *Pastor-Fido,* as having more of nature in it, and being almost wholly clear from the wretched affectation of learning. . . . It is no wonder that rolling down through so many barbarous ages, from the spring of Virgil, it bears along with it the filth and ordures of the Goths and Vandals. Neither will I mention Monsieur Fontenelle, the living glory of the French. It is enough for him to have excelled his master, Lucian, without attempting to compare our miserable age with that of Virgil or Theocritus. Let me only add, for his reputation,

si Pergama dextra
Defendi possent, etiam hac defensa fuissent.

But Spenser being master of our northern dialect, and skilled in Chaucer's English, has so exactly imitated the Dorick of Theocritus, that his love is a perfect image of that passion which God infused into both sexes, before it was corrupted with knowledge of arts, and the ceremonies of what we call good manners.

Classical the Elegy remains, with traces of its Theocritean origin, for many a long year; and, as we shall see hereafter, the stigmata of its origin survive even to this day. Ben Jonson's Ode *To the Immortal Memory and Friendship of that noble pair, Sir Lucius Cary and Sir H. Morison* is thoroughly classical, albeit addressed to an actual and named English gentleman.

> Call, noble Lucius, then for wine,
> And let thy looks with gladness shine:
> Accept this garland, plant it on thy head,
> And think—nay, know—thy Morison's not dead.
>
> He leap'd the present age,
> Possest with holy rage
> To see that bright eternal Day
> Of which we Priests and Poets say
> Such truths as we expect for happy men;
> And there he lives with memory—and Ben
>
> *Jonson*: who sung this of him, ere he went
> Himself to rest,
> Or tast a part of that full joy he meant
> To have exprest
> In this bright Asterism
> Where it were friendship's schism—

Were not his Lucius long with us to tarry—
  To separate these twy
  Lights, the Dioscuri,
And keep the one half from his Harry.
But fate doth so alternate the design,
Whilst that in Heav'n, this light on earth must shine.

  And shine as you exalted are!
  Two names of friendship, but one star:

—Cowley's "Ledaean stars" again, Castor and Pollux,
the Dioscuri—always the emblem of twin friendship
translated to the stars.

  The classical tradition holds again with Jonson's
friend Drummond of Hawthornden throughout his
many laments for his lost mistress.

  Alexis, here she stay'd; among these pines,
  Sweet hermitress, she did alone repair . . .

Hear it in two short pieces:

Her Passing

  The beauty and the life
    Of life's and beauty's fairest paragon
  —O tears! O grief!—hung at a feeble thread
  To which pale Atropos had set her knife;
    The soul with many a groan
    Had left each outward part,
  And now did take his last leave of the heart:
  Naught else did want, save death, ev'n to be dead;
  When the afflicted band about her bed,
  Seeing so fair him come in lips, cheeks, eyes,
  Cried, *"Ah! and can Death enter Paradise?"*

—and the following, so exquisitely playing with a re-membered glimpse of the poet's lost one—

MADRIGAL

Like the Idalian queen,
   Her hair about her eyne,
With neck and breasts' ripe apples to be seen,
   At first glance of the morn
In Cyprus' gardens gathering those fair flow'rs
   Which of her blood were born,
I saw, but fainting saw, my paramours.
The Graces naked danced about the place,
   The winds and trees amazed
   With silence on her gazed,
The flowers did smile, like those upon her face;
And as their aspen stalks those fingers band,
   That she might read my case,
A hyacinth I wish'd me in her hand.

(Concerning which piece of loveliness, risking heresy, I will dare to say that it contains a purer, clearer under-standing of the classical idea—the essential thing in itself—than almost any page of Keats—even of Keats.)

The Spenserian concept of Pastoral, including Elegy, continues, with fall and rise of vivacity, through Spen-ser's imitator Basse, through Herrick, through Phineas Fletcher, through William Browne and others, down to Pope; who in *A Discourse on Pastoral Poetry* prefixed in 1704 or thereabouts to his own early attempts, thus defines the attenuated thing:

A Pastoral is an imitation of the action of a shepherd, or one considered under that character. The form of this imitation is dramatic, or narrative, or mixed of both; the fable simple, the manners not too polite nor too rustic; the thoughts are plain, yet admit a little quickness and passion, but that short and flowing: the expression humble, yet as pure as the language will afford; neat, but not florid; easy, and yet lively. In short, the fable, manners, thoughts, and expressions are full of the greatest simplicity in nature.

The complete character of this poem consists in simplicity, brevity, and delicacy; the two first of which render an Eclogue natural, and the last delightful.

Here are a few lines of his own illustrative of what Pope meant at that time—

> But see! where Daphne wond'ring mounts on high
> Above the clouds, above the starry sky!
> Eternal beauties grace the shining scene,
> Fields ever fresh, and groves for ever green!
> There while you rest in Amaranthine bow'rs,
> Or from those meads select unfading flow'rs,
> Behold us kindly, who your name implore,
> Daphne, our Goddess, and our grief no more!

Pope also wrote "A Sacred Eclogue" on the Messiah, in imitation of Virgil's fourth Eclogue, the famous *Polio*: a performance which suffers by comparison with its original for several reasons apart from the simple one that while *Polio*—

> Ultima Cumaei venit iam carminis aetas—

deals pathetically with the future, Messiah prophesies that which had been an accomplished fact for seventeen hundred years.

But Pope lived to learn and do better; as in his *Elegy to the Memory of an Unfortunate Lady,* that begins—

What beck'ning ghost, along the moonlight shade
Invites my steps, and points to yonder glade?

and ends so nobly—

So peaceful rests, without a stone, a name,
What once had beauty, titles, wealth, and fame.
How loved, how honour'd once, avails thee not,
To whom related, or by whom begot;
A heap of dust alone remains of thee,
'Tis all thou art, and all the proud shall be!
Poets themselves must fall, like those they sung,
Deaf the praised ear, and mute the tuneful tongue.
Ev'n he, whose soul now melts in mournful lays,
Shall shortly want the gen'rous tear he pays;
Then from his closing eyes thy form shall part,
And the last pang shall tear thee from his heart;
Life's idle business at one gasp be o'er,
The Muse forgot, and thou beloved no more!

II

But we must now go back to the entrance of a second
channel through which the Elegy flowed in the seventeenth century. That channel was opened, of course, by
John Donne.

Donne's reputation has come to its own of late: one
might almost say that he has become a fashion again.
But he went his way like a great Sower, scattering seed:
of which some fell by the wayside, some on stony places,
some among thorns: yet a residue on good ground,
whereon it brought forth fruit—much in the seventeenth
century; and good aftermath yet in our own day.
Therefore, without indulging in quotations, I shall
assume you to be fairly well acquainted with his Elegies,

in places so grandly impressive, in others so dark and fuliginous, yet altogether—I dare to say—so vapid in trivialities when we set them either beside his early love-poems or his later tremendous Sermons. As for their "conceits," we know that Donne's mind habitually dwelt on death with its accessories and trappings—the coffin, the cerecloth, the charnel-house, the worm. Such conceits as he evokes from his grisly meditations, or spins around them, came to him naturally and therefore pardonably. But when his successors imitate him in these as in other of his peculiarities, lacking his inspiration, they are apt merely to offend us.

Take, for instance, a few lines from an Elegy by William Cartwright (1611-1643)—*To the Memory of a Shipwrack't Virgin*—

> Whether thy well-shap'd parts now scatter'd far
> Asunder into Treasure parted are:
> Whether thy Tresses, now to Amber grown,
> Still cast a softer day where they are shown, etc.

You may ask, if I dislike this, how can I justify Ariel's dirge?

> Full fathom five thy father lies,
> Of his bones are coral made:
> Those are pearls that were his eyes,
> Nothing of him that doth fade. . . .

To which I answer that *The Tempest* is a fairy story and Ariel's imagery removed from present tears: but Cartwright's imagery is inappropriate to an actual human occasion. His concluding address to the fated ship is better, but still artificial—

And thou unfaithful ill-compacted Pine,
That in her Nuptials did refuse to shine,
Blaze in her Pile!

Crashaw again—a true poet—abounds, as you know,
in similar conceits which we condemn not so much
because they are conceits as because they miss "coming
off," the occasion being too serious for them, or at least
too intimate.   Take for instance his lines upon Mr.
Staninough's death, beginning—

Dear relics of a dislodged soul, whose lack
Makes many a mourning paper put on black,
O, stay awhile, ere thou draw in thy head,
And wind thyself up close in thy cold bed!

III

I said enough just now—perhaps more than enough—
in defence of the artifice of the classically-derived Elegy.
In fact all true art must use artifice, avoiding its natural
danger, which is artificiality.

Let it be confessed that *Lycidas* in places comes perilously near to falling into this trap.   Let it be even noted
that a number of our English Eclogues, classically
inspired, have been written by poets not passionately
attached by ties of blood or parentage to the dead ones
they lament.   As we have seen, there is no reason to
suppose Milton to have been overwhelmed by the death
of Edward King.   Shelley composed one of the noblest
Elegies in our language upon Keats, with whom in life
he had small intimacy and perhaps less sympathy.   I
recall here a stray allusion to Wycherley in a letter of
Dryden's addressed to John Dennis.

Jupiter and Juno, as the poets tell us, made Tiresias their umpire in a certain merry dispute, which fell out in heaven betwixt them. Tiresias, you know, had been of both sexes, and therefore was a proper judge; our friend Mr. Wycherley is full as competent an arbitrator: he has been a bachelor, and marry'd man, and is now a widower.

But, still as we study the seventeenth century, we find yet a third channel of Elegy, through which flows—though in no great volume to be sure—a stream of personal grief, simple, intense, run straight from the heart, and in its immediacy independent alike of conceits and of Theocritean scenery. Consider this from Bishop King's *Exequy* on his wife:

> Accept, thou shrine of my dead saint,
> Instead of dirges this complaint;
> And for sweet flowers to crown thy herse
> Receive a strew of weeping verse
> From thy griev'd friend, whom thou might'st see
> Quite melted into tears for thee.
>   Dear loss! since thy untimely fate,
> My task hath been to meditate
> On thee, on thee! Thou art the book,
> The library whereon I look,
> Tho' almost blind. For thee, lov'd clay,
> I languish out, not live, the day . . .
>   Sleep on, my Love, in thy cold bed
> Never to be disquieted!
> My last good-night! Thou wilt not wake
> Till I thy fate shall overtake:
> Till age, or grief, or sickness must
> Marry my body to that dust
> It so much loves; and fill the room
> My heart keeps empty in thy tomb.

Stay for me there: I will not fail
To meet thee in that hollow vale.
And think not much of my delay:
I am already on the way,
And follow thee with all the speed
Desire can make, or sorrows breed.
Each minute is a short degree
And every hour a step towards thee . . .
   'Tis true—with shame and grief I yield—
Thou, like the van, first took'st the field;
And gotten hast the victory
In thus adventuring to die
Before me, whose more years might crave
A just precedence in the grave.
But hark! my pulse, like a soft drum,
Beats my approach, tells thee I come;
And slow howe'er my marches be,
I shall at last sit down by thee.
   The thought of this bids me go on
And wait my dissolution
With hope and comfort. Dear—forgive
The crime!—I am content to live
Divided, with but half a heart,
Till we shall meet and never part.

Not entirely unmarred by conceits, yet lifted by an emotion that transcends them, are Vaughan's lines on his *Friends Departed*.

They are all gone into the world of light!
   And I alone sit ling'ring here; . . .

Dear, beauteous Death! the jewel of the Just,
   Shining nowhere, but in the dark;
What mysteries do lie beyond thy dust,
   Could man outlook that mark!

He that hath found some fledged bird's nest may know,
  At first sight, if the bird be flown;
But what fair well or grove he sings in now,
  That is to him unknown.

Let us pause here for a moment on those last two
lines—

  But what fair well or grove he sings in now,
    That is to him unknown—

to note a disability, or rather a double disability under
which the Elegy, in common with some other verse-
forms, must suffer by the Englishing of a classical
model. A Sicilian Greek, or a Mantuan, would have
found no difficulty, at any rate in legend, in connecting
the departed spirit with some particular grove or well.
It would have been a grove or well consecrated to some
god or demi-god or other from whom either the poet or
the lamented friend traditionally derived his ancestry.
In England, with our accepted religion of one unseen
God in Trinity, we have none of these special *genii loci,*
president deities of this or that mountain, glade, river
or river source. We invent a "Father Thames" or a
"Camus, reverend Sire"; but we have not that intimacy
which the Greeks and Latins had with *their* deities, who
were sublimated men and women, of like passions with
themselves. This difficulty has commonly been felt by
our sacred poets, and even more commonly by their
critics. And Doctor Johnson was almost driven to conclude that the noble employments of pious meditation—
faith, thanksgiving, repentance, supplication—could not
find utterance in poetry; that contemplative piety, or
the intercourse between God and the human soul, could
not be poetical; in other words, that religion and poetry
can never quite agree. Wither and Quarles, for example,

were Bavius and Maevius in the century that followed
them. But Wither at any rate, in his honest if somewhat pedestrian way, had never a doubt that poetry
could bring religion home to everyday life, and indeed
found its highest sanction in doing this. As Charles
Lamb says,

The praises of poetry have often been sung in ancient and
in modern times: strange powers have been ascribed to it of
influence over animate and inanimate auditors; its force over
fascinated crowds has been acknowledged: but before Wither
no one ever celebrated its power *at home,* the wealth and the
strength which this divine gift confers upon its possessor.
Fame, and that too after death, was all which hitherto the
poets had promised themselves from their art. It seems to
have been left to Wither to discover, that poetry was a present
possession as well as a rich reversion, and that the muse had
promise of both lives—of this and of that which was to
come.

In writing his consolatory hymns in *Hallelujah*—
hymns which he intended to be generally applicable and
of use in any house of mourning—and especially in his
captions for them—Wither, indeed, sometimes treads
perilously near the edge of the ridiculous: as in hymns
XXVII and XXVIII—

*For a Widower, or a Widow deprived of a
loving Yoke-fellow*

This hymn teacheth a moderate expressing of their natural
passions, and remembers them of things not to be forgotten in
their sorrow.

*For a Widower, or a Widow delivered from a
troublesome Yoke-fellow*

Because deliverance from a troublesome yoke-fellow is a benefit neither to be despised nor indiscreetly rejoiced in; this Hymn teacheth with what moderation, with what tenderness of heart, and with what desire we should be affected in such cases.

But the former of these has stanzas well worth our remembering.

> The voice which I did more esteem
> Than music in her sweetest key,
> Those eyes which unto me did seem
> More comfortable than the day;
>   Those now by me, as they have been,
>   Shall never more be heard or seen;
> But what I once enjoyed in them
> Shall seem hereafter as a dream.
>
> Lord! keep me faithful to the trust
> Which my dear spouse reposed in me,
> To him now dead preserve me just
> In all that should performèd be;
>   For though our being man and wife
>   Extended only to this life,
> Yet neither life nor death should end
> The being of a faithful friend.

IV

We have now, dismissing the fashion of "conceits," brought the classical and the direct Elegy down to the age of Pope.

The classical or Pastoral Elegy soon falls thereafter into contempt, mainly through the insipidities of Ambrose Philips, a short specimen of whose art from his lament for *Albino* (otherwise the Duke of Gloucester,

one of the many untimely blossoms of Queen Anne and
Prince George of Denmark) may serve our purpose
here.

> Sent into life, alas! how short thy stay:
> How sweet the rose! How speedy to decay!
> Can we forget, Albino dear, thy knell,
> Sad-sounding wide from every village bell?
> Can we forget how sorely Albion moan'd,
> That hills, and dales, and rocks in echo groan'd,
> Presaging future woe, when for our crimes
> We lost Albino, pledge of peaceful times—

and so on. Men like Prior and Gay, inheriting the trick
of this but endowed with a sense of humour, could carry
on the Pastoral only by lampooning it or by diverting
the trick to polite and half satirical verse. They found
the Elegy itself by its nature more difficult to treat
ludicrously, but diverted it in a man-of-the-world
fashion. Prior for instance wrote an Elegy *For His
Own Monument,* "as Doctors give physic by way of
prevention."

> This verse little polish'd, though mighty sincere,
>   Sets neither his titles nor merit to view,
> It says, that his relics collected lie here,
>   And no mortal yet knows too if this may be true.

> If his bones lie in earth, roll in sea, fly in air,
>   To Fate we must yield, and the thing is the same,
> And if passing thou giv'st him a smile, or a tear,
>   He cares not—yet pr'ythee be kind to his FAME.

By far his best effort in this style however being his
incomparable *Jinny the Just,* so full of tender regret

beneath its smiles. One feels concerning these men as Walter Pater makes the supposed narrator of *A Prince of Court Painters* feel concerning Antony Watteau:

   And yet, methinks Antony Watteau reproduces that gallant world, those patched and powdered ladies and fine cavaliers, so much to its own satisfaction, partly because he despises it: if this be a possible condition of excellent artistic production.

   But, for the poem:

Jinny the Just

Releas'd from the noise of the Butcher and Baker
Who, my old Friends be thanked, did seldom forsake her
And from the soft Duns of my Landlord the Quaker

From chiding the Footmen and watching the Lasses,
From Nell that burn'd Milk, and Tom that broke Glasses
(Sad mischiefs thro which a good housekeeper passes!)

From some real Care but more fancy'd vexation,
From a life party Colour'd half reason half passion,
Here lies after all the best Wench in the Nation.

From the Rhine to the Po, from the Thames to the Rhone—
Joanna or Janneton, Jinny or Joan—
Twas all one to her by what name She was known.

For the Idiom of words very little She heeded:
Provided the Matter She drove at succeeded
She took and gave Languages just as She needed.

So for Kitching and Market, for bargain & Sale,
She paid English or Dutch or french down on the Nail—
But in telling a Story she sometimes did fail.

Then begging Excuse as She happen'd to Stammer
With respect to her betters but none to her Grammer,
Her blush helpt her out and her Jargon became her

Her Habit and Mein she endeavor'd to frame
To the different Gout of the place where She came:
Her outside stil chang'd, but her inside the same

At the Hague in her Slippers & hair as the Mode is—
At Paris all Falbalow'd fine as a Goddess
And at censuring London in smock sleeves and Bodice—

She order'd Affairs that few people cou'd tell
In what part about her that mixture did dwell
Of Vrough or Mistress, or Medemoiselle

For her Sirname and race let the Heraults e'en Answer.
Her own proper worth was enough to advance her;
And he who lik'd *her,* little valu'd her Grandsire.

But from what House so ever her lineage may come
I wish my own Jinny but out of her Tomb,
Tho all her relations were there in her Room!

Of such terrible beauty She never cou'd boast
As with absolute Sway o'er all hearts rules the roast,
When J—— bawls out to the Chair for a Toast.

But of good Household Features her Person was made;
Nor by Faction cry'd up nor of Censure afraid;
And her beauty was rather for Use than Parade.

Her Blood so well mix't and flesh so well Pasted
That tho her Youth faded her Comliness lasted,
The blew was wore off but the Plum was well tasted.

Less smooth than her Skin and less white than her breast
Was this pollisht stone beneath which she lyes prest.
Stop, Reader and Sigh while thou thinkst on the rest!

With a just trim of Virtue her Soul was endu'd:
Not affectedly Pious nor secretly lewd,
She cut even between the Cocquet and the Prude.

Her Will with her Duty so equally stood
That seldom oppos'd She was commonly good,
And did pritty well, doing just what she wou'd.

Declining all Pow'r she found means to perswade,
Was then most regarded when most she Obey'd;
The Mistress in truth when she seem'd but the Maid.

Such care of her own proper Actions She took
That on other folks lives She had no time to look:
So Censure and Praise were struck out of her Book.

Her thought stil confin'd to its own little Sphere,
She minded not who did Excell or did Err
But just as the matter related to *her*.

Then too when her Private Tribunal was rear'd
Her Mercy so mix'd with her judgment appear'd
That her Foes were condemn'd & her friends always clear'd.

Her Religion so well with her learning did suite
That, in Practice sincere, and in Controverse Mute,
She shew'd She knew better to live than dispute,

Some parts of the Bible by heart She recited,
And much in historical Chapters delighted:
But in points about Faith She was something short sighted.

So Notions and modes She refer'd to the Schools;
And in matters of Conscience adher'd to Two Rules—
To advise with no Biggots, and jest with no Fools.

And scrupling but little, enough she believ'd:
By Charity ample smal sins She retriev'd:
And, when she had New Cloaths, She always receiv'd.

Thus stil whilst her Morning unseen fled away
In ord'ring the Linnen and making the Tea,
That she scarce cou'd have time for the Psalms of the Day;

And while after Dinner the Night came so soon
That half she propos'd very seldom was done,
With twenty god bless Me's how this day is gone!

While she read and Accounted & payd & abated
Eat and drank, Play'd & Work't, laught & Cry'd, lov'd &
    hated,
As answer'd the end of her being Created.

In the midst of her Age came a cruel Desease
Which neither her Julips nor recepts cou'd appease—
So down dropt her Clay, may her Soul be at peace!

Retire from this Sepulchre all the Prophane:
You that love for Debauch or that marry for gain:
Retire least Ye trouble the Manes of J——!

But Thou that know'st Love above Intrest or lust,
Strew the Myrtle and Rose on this once belov'd Dust,
And shed one pious tear upon Jinny the Just.

Tread soft on her Grave, and do right to her honor:
Let neither rude hand nor ill Tongue light upon her:
Do all the smal Favors that now can be done her.

And when what Thou lik't shal return to her Clay,
For so I'm perswaded she must do one Day,
What ever fantastic J—— Asgil may say.

When as I have done now, thou shalt set up a Stone
For something however distinguisht or known,
May some Pious Friend the Misfortune bemoan,
And make thy Concern, by reflexion, his own.

Goldsmith writes an Elegy on a mad dog. Another on a female pawnbroker. Gray *On a Favourite Cat, Drowned in a Tub of Gold Fishes.*

V

But with Gray we come back to the *Country Church-yard* and to more serious business.

Gray had written an Elegiac sonnet upon his friend Richard West (d. 1742) in which Wordsworth and Coleridge were afterwards at pains to separate the lines of true feeling from those of false poetic diction.

> In vain to me the smiling mornings shine,
>   And reddening Phoebus lifts his golden fire;
> The birds in vain their amorous descant join,
>   Or cheerful fields resume their green attire.

A letter of his to Horace Walpole, dated from Cambridge, Feb. 11, 1751, pretty well indicates his attitude towards his ever famous Elegy.

Yesterday I had the Misfortune of receiving a letter from certain Gentlemen (as their Bookseller expresses it) who have taken the Magazine of Magazines into their hands. They tell me that an ingenious Poem call'd "Reflections in a Country-Churchyard" has been communicated to them, which they are printing forthwith: that they are inform'd that the *excellent* Author of it is I by name, and they beg not only his *Indulgence,* but *the Honour of his Correspondence* etc. As I am not at all disposed to be either so indulgent or so correspondent as they desire, I have but one bad way to escape the Honour they would inflict upon me, and therefore am obliged to desire you would make Dodsley print it immediately (which may be done in less than a week's time) from your Copy, but without my name, in what Form is

most convenient for him, but in his best Paper and Character.
He must correct the Press himself, and print it without any
Interval between the stanzas, because the sense is in some
places continued beyond them, and the Title must be, *Elegy,
wrote in a Country Church-yard*. If he would add a line or
two to say it came into his Hands by Accident, I should like
it better. . . .

P.S. If Dodsley don't do this immediately he may as well
let it alone.

So it was published, in five days from the above date,
as a quarto pamphlet price sixpence: prefixed with an
Advertisement in which Horace Walpole duly said that
it had come into his hands by accident.

Now concerning Gray's masterpiece you may object
to me that since I call it (as you would be right in
guessing) undeniably classical, it upsets a great deal of
what I have been saying about the classical Elegy; since
here we have no gods, no shepherds, no classical allusions. But the objection would be no more than specious:
for Gray deliberately excludes these because he tells of a
country churchyard and in it deliberately meditates on
the innominate dead, who were (some of them) actual
shepherds—which is a very different thing from writing
of the Countess of Pembroke as a shepherdess or of
Edward King and Arthur Hugh Clough as shepherds.
He has to level deliberately "the boast of heraldry, the
pomp of power" with the poor crooked scythe and spade;
and, having levelled them, to lift the common dignity of
death alike above turfed mound and pyramid. Deliberately therefore he strips away all decorations—the frieze
of god and shepherd, of lover and pursued, the wreathed
ivy, and the lilies, the pipes and timbrels and wild
ecstasy that Keats found on *his* Grecian Urn. But the

true *form* of that Urn reveals itself all the more clearly as monumental, and its substance as marble.

We have seen what Doctor Johnson thought of Gray's performance. Johnson himself wrote an Elegy

On the Death of Mr. Robert Levet, a Practiser in Physic

in which we find a plenty of that "robust common sense" for which it is usual to praise Johnson even to weariness; the only trouble with it in this connection being that robust common sense is about the last quality anyone should require of an Elegy. Johnson, be it remembered, was the widower of a plain wife, the anniversary of whose death he punctually observed; he had no children; he had many friends to whose interests, while they lived, he was sincerely devoted; he rejoiced in their company and would go to any extent of trouble in their service. But he did not mourn them when they were dead, having a philosophy of his own about friendship. Boswell held that friendship, "the wine of life," should, like a well-stocked cellar, be continually renewed; and it is consolatory to think that although we can seldom add what will equal the generous *first-growths* of our youth, yet friendship becomes insensibly old in much less time than is commonly imagined, and not many years are required to make it very mellow and pleasant. Johnson agreed with this, and told Sir Joshua Reynolds, "If a man does not make new acquaintance as he advances through life, he will soon find himself left alone. A man, sir, should keep his friendship *in constant repair*." His lines on Levet will indicate how far his common sense was prepared to go, when his "Social comforts dropped away."

Well tried through many a varying year,
  See Levet to the grave descend,
Officious, innocent, sincere,
  Of ev'ry friendless name the friend.

Yet still he fills affection's eye,
  Obscurely wise and coarsely kind;
Nor, letter'd Arrogance, deny
  Thy praise to merit unrefined.

When fainting nature call'd for aid,
  And hov'ring death prepared the blow,
His vig'rous remedy display'd
  The pow'r of art without the show.

In Misery's darkest cavern known,
  His useful care was ever nigh,
Where hopeless Anguish pour'd his groan.
  And lonely Want retired to die.

No summons mock'd by chill delay,
  No petty gain disdain'd by pride;
The modest wants of ev'ry day
  The toil of ev'ry day supplied.

His virtues walk'd their narrow round,
  Nor made a pause, nor left a void;
And sure th' Eternal Master found
  The single talent well employ'd.

The busy day, the peaceful night,
  Unfelt, uncounted, glided by;
His frame was firm—his powers were bright,
  Though now his eightieth year was nigh.

Then with no fiery throbbing pain,
  No cold gradations of decay,
Death broke at once the vital chain,
  And freed his soul the nearest way.

But the passionate direct Elegy is not far from its resurrection. It revives in Cowper's most poignant lines *On the Receipt of My Mother's Picture out of Norfolk:* it revives in Burns's *Lament for James, Earl of Glencairn—*

> The bridegroom may forget the bride
>   Was made his wedded wife yestreen;
> The monarch may forget the crown
>   That on his head an hour has been;
> The mother may forget the child
>   That smiles sae sweetly on her knee;
> But I'll remember thee, Glencairn,
>   And a' that thou hast done for me!

It revives in Wordsworth's *Lucy*—that heart-subduing sequence; it is revived by Byron and by many another.

VI

And almost simultaneously—or with the beginning of the nineteenth century—the *classical* form revives. We meet with the tradition again in *Adonais,* which some hold to be the greatest Elegy in the language. For a confession, I hold that *Adonais* would be a better poem if a shorter, and could at any rate willingly spare the stanzas beginning "Or go to Rome!" which surely come as anticlimax—not a falling close but a rhetorical anticlimax—after the glorious five stanzas that start with "Peace, peace! he is not dead . . ." and include

> He has outsoared the shadow of our night;
> Envy and calumny and hate and pain,
> And that unrest which men miscall delight,
> Can touch him not and torture not again;
> From the contagion of the world's slow stain

He is secure, and now can never mourn
A heart grown cold, a head grown gray in vain;
Nor, when the spirit's self has ceased to burn,
With sparkless ashes load an unlamented urn.

For the Roman business, I think Byron does that sort of thing better: it has almost a smack of University Prize Composition. (But this is parenthetical, and Doctor Johnson would have shortened *Lycidas*.) At any rate *Adonais*, with its prefatory quotation from Moschus and its "Lament, Urania!" continues the tradition with careful classical imagery.

No one will deny that Tennyson's *In Memoriam*, evolved after long brooding upon passion, is composed, marmoresque, classical. In Arnold's *Scholar Gypsy* the classics lift their voice unashamed.

Go, for they call you, shepherd, from the hill;
Go, shepherd and unloose the wattled cotes.

Their voices are lifted again in Swinburne's lament for Baudelaire—*Ave atque Vale*—

For thee, O now a silent soul, my brother,
Take at my hands this garland, and farewell.
Thin is the leaf and chill the wintry smell,
And chill the solemn earth, a fatal mother,
With sadder than the Niobean womb,
And in the hollow of her breasts a tomb.
Content thee, howsoe'er, whose days are done;
There lies not any troublous thing before,
Nor sight nor sound to war against thee more,
For whom all winds are quiet as the sun,
    All waters as the shore.

It continues to our living Laureate's elegy *On a Lady whom grief for her Betrothed killed.*

> Cloke her in ermine, for the night is cold,
> And wrap her warmly, for the night is long.
> In pious hands the flaming torches hold,
> While her attendants, chosen from among
>   Her faithful virgin throng,
>   May lay her in her cedar litter,
> Decking her coverlet with sprigs of gold,
> Roses, and lilies white that best befit her.
>
> Let the priests go before, array'd in white,
> And let the dark-stoled minstrels follow slow,
> Next they that bear her, honour'd on this night,
> And then the maidens, in a double row,
>   Each singing soft and low,
> And each on high a torch upstaying:
> Unto her lover lead her forth with light,
> With music, and with singing, and with praying.

VII

Also, and alongside great rhetorical laments such as Tennyson's *Ode on the Death of the Duke of Wellington,* the simple direct form of Elegy survived through the nineteenth century to this day. My time is almost up, or I might quote you specimens from Roden Noel's *A Little Child's Monument* or T. E. Brown's *Aber Stations,* each a father's threnody over a lost son. But I will content myself with one poem and with that conclude. It is by William Barnes, who has hitherto missed his true place in general esteem through his own perversity—that is through over-laying his poetry with a monstrous philological spelling intended to convey the *nuances* of Dorsetshire speech. The poem is entitled

The Wife Alost.   I have transferred it here into simple English, and shall endeavour to convey, not too broadly, the West-country accent as I read it to you.

Since I no more do see your face,
    Upstairs or down below,
I'll sit me in the lonesome place,
    Where flat-bough'd beech do grow;
Below the beeches' bough, my love,
    Where you did never come,
An' I don't look to meet you now,
    As I do look at home.

Since you no more be at my side,
    In walks in summer het,
I'll go alone where mist do ride,
    Dro' trees a'drippen wet;
Below the rain-wet bough, my love,
    Where you did never come,
An' I don't grieve to miss ye now,
    As I do grieve at home.

Since now beside my dinner-board
    Your voice do never sound,
I'll eat the bit I can afford
    A'field upon the ground;
Below the darksome bough, my love,
    Where you did never dine,
An' I don't grieve to miss ye now,
    As I at home do pine.

Since I do miss your voice and face
    In prayer at eventide,
I'll pray with one sad voice for grace
    To go where you do bide;

Above the tree and bough, my love,
Where you be gone afore,
An' be awaiten' for me now,
To come for evermore.

There today we leave the English Elegy, Gentlemen, having traced and discussed its immanence and continuity in two forms, the decorative and the direct. It is not for me to suggest that one or other of these is worthier of the future, or even that the future may not give birth to a third form distinct from either. From this desk I have never preached any law for literature but the obedience of faith: but of this I am sure, that, however its form may change, the function of Elegy must abide, since it renders a permanent service of its own to human life. So long as man exists he must always be asking the question of the Emperor Hadrian to his soul

Animula, vagula, blandula!
Hospes comesque corporis,
Quae nunc abibis in loca?
Pallidula, rigida, nudula.

even as he can never escape the implications of his own transience.

The summer air o' this green hill
'v a-heav'd in bosoms now all still,
An' all their hopes an' all their tears
Be unknown things of other years.

To such questions, to such meditations, the Elegy will always minister, as to

Infinite passion, and the pain
Of finite hearts that yearn.

NOTE. In the foregoing Lectures I have tried to indicate the main source and divergent streams of the Elegy in England without breaking the tale by interposing Mantuan (for example) and Marot, and Spenser's debt to them. A discussion of that debt more properly belongs to a study of the Eclogue in general, and at any rate, as I think, has such secondary value as, rightly enough in its place, belongs to a close examination of the filter-beds between the upper and lower waters of a genuine stream.

I have also omitted all discussion of *Pearl,* that amazing and phenomenal English Elegy of the fourteenth century; and this simply because my ignorance, after reading what many scholars have written, allows me still to wonder what was its ancestry and what its progeny. With that confession I must leave this medieval *tour de force,* as in a boat I should avoid a sharp unaccountable rock in a smoothly running channel.

THE JOURNALS OF
DOROTHY WORDSWORTH (I)

I

I SHALL begin by positing to you, Gentlemen, a question which bears immediately upon my talk this morning and a fortnight hence, and not without opportunity, since it was raised for all of us, a week or two back, by the extreme indelicacy of our newspaper Press during the week after the death of that great and simple countryman, Thomas Hardy.

I had the privilege to know him and be a listener to much intimate talk; for no better reason than that I knew the countryside of that first courtship of his, which his memory fondly idealised—places, names, folk departed or in few surviving. And I will swear that nothing could have been falser or unjuster to all that Hardy ever meant, wished or stood for than the strangling sobs of the British Press in Westminster Abbey over the writer of *Under the Greenwood Tree.*

I propose this question to you, Gentlemen—in dealing with the work and lives of our authors we are always having to face it—before I dare to open the door upon a chamber that for every scholar in the writings of her time should be hallowed—the soul's sanctuary of the incomparable Dorothy Wordsworth.

But first let us have it out (I say) as a general question.

54

Like most human instincts, that which prompts us to be curious concerning the lives of great authors, as of other great men, is healthy enough if temperately controlled. I think, making a guess, that the great man himself may just as instinctively hate it, nay *should* hate it and seek to cover up his tracks, wishing to live by his work and not concurrently by advertisement of his private generosities, frailties or foibles. Of Thackeray, for example, it is recorded that, one day, holding up a recently published volume of biography, he solemnly charged his daughters, "Let there be no nonsense of this kind after my death"—an adjuration piously observed, with the result that no standard biography of Thackeray has appeared to this day. The loss (if we choose to call it a loss) has not checked an endless irrigation of reminiscence and chat about Thackeray in critical "Studies" and "Introductions": so that on the whole he has fared no better than Charles Dickens, whose *Life* by John Forster is at any rate a solid piece of work, solidly documented and honest of purpose to be challenged, after all, by scandal.

II

Let me try to set out the account squarely, putting away my own prejudice, which is all on Thackeray's side— for my own ghost, if ever I have one, will certainly hate and haunt anyone who should hereafter attempt a memoir of the lecturer today addressing you. Tomorrow, or next day, he will be dead and all covered up save the little spark he may haply transmit to your memory: and so best, I say most earnestly. But—to put the one side of the case as soberly as possible—all biography and all autobiography suffer from this, that no man can tell the truth about another's soul, and no man dares to tell it of his own. Of autobiographies I suppose those of Messieurs Cellini, Casanova and Rousseau would be considered as about the frankest, exposing as they do an indecent amount of personality. Actually, to anyone who studies what they reveal against what they wrap away and hide, whether of event or passion, there is little to choose between them as artistic fakes. They will not stand a moment's test against John Bunyan's *Grace Abounding*. But now comes along the improving biographer. He is (say) the late Mr. Froude, and he takes this very man Bunyan and this very book—with what result let the late Mark Rutherford summarise—

Mr. Froude was most unfitted to write the *Life of Bunyan:* anybody reading *his* Bunyan and knowing nothing about the author of *The Pilgrim's Progress* save what Mr. Froude tells him, would imagine that Bunyan was a spiritually dyspeptic person, over-hung all his days with the gloomy shadow of insoluble Calvinism. That is what Mr. Froude would have been had he, to use an Irishism, been Bunyan.

So there you have the proper snare of Biography: the perpetual temptation to interpret your hero in terms of yourself—as Carlyle, for example, interpreted Cromwell.

Now and then, as in Boswell, you get a biographer, at once sedulous and intelligent, who completely bows his mind to his task and so contrives that his own vanity subserves his task; or, as in Mrs. Gaskell's *Life of Charlotte Brontë,* an unselfish author, skilled to write, who produces a little masterpiece with no afterthought at all behind truth and duty to the memory of a friend. But will our Paul Prys be content with that admittedly fair picture? No, they will not. Private writing-desks and drawers must be ransacked, their contents printed, that the world after her death may debate how far this girl was in love with a teacher in Brussels.

III

So much for the one side : and its upholders may count the world lucky that it knows nothing of Homer, little more of Virgil, of Horace just so much as he has chosen to tell us, and of our own Shakespeare a very small definite amount which, thanks to laborious efforts to expand it, promises (it may be hoped) to diminish, in Heaven's good time, to nothing at all.

But take the instinct : and, for example, Shakespeare. As I have said elsewhere, doubtless it were a counsel of perfection to accept his work simply, gratefully, and to let the man go. But he has meant so much to us. . . . We demand, as Jacob, after wrestling all night with the angel, demanded :

Tell me, I pray thee, thy name. And he said, Wherefore is it that thou dost ask after my name? And he blessed him there.

Yet we crave to know, and who (say you) in the end thinks worse of these men for knowing? We regret (say) certain passages in the letters of Keats to Fanny Brawne. Do they really hurt our thoughts of Keats, or impair anything that was honest in them? For a confession, I detest with a peculiar detestation all the disputes and so-called revelations concerning Byron's break with his wife. Yet there is your Byron : and if you don't know something of the tragedy, why is the man trailing over Europe the pageant of his bleeding heart? Yes, of Byron, speaking as one prejudiced on the side of reticence, I hold up my hands and surrender. For here we have a poet of undoubted genius, persistently, vociferously, shouting his private anguish while either impossibly ignorant of the cause or deliberately hiding it from the audience he invokes. Does not such a poem as *Manfred* go, as far as it challenges, to excuse the curiosity it provokes?

Let me recall to you the story told by Plato, in the Fourth Book of the *Republic,* concerning one Leontius, son of Aglaion: who, coming up one day from the Piraeus, under the outside of the north wall, observed some corpses of malefactors scattered and putrefying about the place of execution. He felt a craving to inspect them, with a battling abhorrence. For a time he struggled and covered his eyes, and then, beaten and forcing them open, ran up to the carrion, crying, "Look, you beasts! Take your fill of the delectable vision!"

IV

Let us abate this curiosity upon two poets, Coleridge and Wordsworth, who, though frank enough with their emotions and sensibilities, never made private woe a public matter as Byron did. The thoughts I shall put before you today, Gentlemen, ultimately concern the private lives of Coleridge and Wordsworth little, if at all. Beyond these they bear on questions ultimate, or so nearly ultimate, as "Can poetry be written to order?" "How far can a poet be *stoked*—so to speak—with punctuality at the domestic hearth?" To put it lightly, "Can the lyric be fed on regular meals?" or "Can the inspired idiot of Plato's conception, as a nuisance in the ideal commonwealth, be reconciled in our minds with a Wordsworthian pawkiness combined with a laureate's bays?" It is testimony at any rate to our national gift for compromise that once, "in our rough island's story," we composed these apparent opposites. But our enquiry, if we pursue it faithfully, may bring us up against one of the most troublesome questions in all criticism, "How, precisely, does a casual passage in Holinshed, or a jotting in somebody's journal, turn by magic touch into unforgettable poetry?"

V

Let me come to these questions in my own way. Some while ago an unknown friend sent me, as a gift, an anonymous volume entitled *Pen and Ink Sketches of Poets, Preachers and Politicians* (London, David Bogue, Fleet Street: Second Edition, Enlarged). Since it is probably unknown to you, as, until a while ago, it was quite unknown to me; and seeing that it contains some (alleged) first-hand and, to my thinking, illuminative depictions of Wordsworth, Coleridge, Southey, Hazlitt, Lamb, Shelley (let be Miss Hannah More, Mrs. Hemans, the two Montgomeries, Ebenezer Elliott) amid its throng of politicians and popular preachers, I shall take leave to spend a few of your minutes in sampling the book.

It behooves one to be very cautious in handling a book of Reminiscences by a writer who withholds his name: and it is his own fault if one suspects certain passages of being literary "fake." Indeed when the author "saw Shelley plain" I confess to a sharp suspicion. For, by his account, walking from Highgate to Hampstead in gathering darkness after a Sunday visit to Coleridge, on the edge of the Heath and by the door of a large house he came on an agitated group—a tall youth with a dead

or insensible female heavy on his arm, and two or three
men-servants half-forcibly resisting his demand that they
should admit the sufferer, administer restoratives and
provide her with a bed at least for the night. In the
midst of the turmoil—for it would seem that everybody
was shouting, and the tall young man loudest of all—
up drives the carriage of the master of the mansion.
Him in the act of alighting—almost before his foot is
on the carriage step—the youth assailed, demanding of
his benevolence cordial waters and a night's shelter for
this female found in syncope on the Heath and borne
hither in his arms. Wine, volatile essences and smelling-
bottles were produced, and—the narrative continues—
"I was gratified to find the suspended animation of the
sufferer itself happily suspended so far as to admit the
entrance of a whole glass of wine, her deglutition of
which seemed to me better than could be expected."
When, however, it came to the demand for a night's
lodging, the man of opulence was (as you would say)
not taking any: and thereupon the youth "vociferated
a philippic against the selfishness of the aristocracy"; he
almost wept, prophesying for England a servile war.
The story concludes:

Meanwhile his female protégée, finding attention directed
from herself to the parties quarrelling, very quietly adjusted
her drapery, seemingly making up her mind that no more
relief was likely to be forthcoming. . . . I believe she proved
to be one of those characters who perambulate London
streets after nightfall, in cold and damp weather, when on
the edge of starvation, or an imposter, or both. . . . It was
not until a week afterwards I heard from a literary friend
living on Hampstead Heath, that this was Shelley. I know
not how he got rid of his reviving companion, for I left the
spot in the midst of the oration. It was a strong practical

illustration of Shelley's theoretical monomania of philan-thropy—that fine, but preposterous excess of humanity that almost drove him melancholy mad over the condition of man.

I admit to a suspicion, on reading this, of dealing with a writer who may have seen Shelley plain but was pre-senting him "twopence coloured." It seemed to me, let me say, just the sort of episode that you or I might invent concerning Shelley. On the whole I gravely distrust this anecdote concerning him.

VI

But let us discriminate: for it is a part of your busi-ness, up here, to learn to discriminate, and no small part of my business to help you.

A book may be faked in part, and yet not all a fake. To me, for example—knowing just what you and I and anyone can gather about Coleridge and Hazlitt—the following few sentences seem to be not only confirmatory but evidence at first-hand.

In his parlour, which was well furnished (a back room and very still, the street being little of a thoroughfare), sate a middle-aged man (Hazlitt), slippered, and in a dishabille indicating recent uprising. . . . He received me with what appeared shyness, or reluctance to be disturbed, but which I afterwards found to be his habit at first meeting. His tones were quite as low as those of Coleridge; when not excited they were almost plaintive or querulous, but his placidity breathed more of unconscious pensiveness than that of his brother thinker, whose complacent meekness always rather savoured of *acting,* at least of a conscious attention to sage or martyr-like bearing, until his aroused enthusiasm broke through all, elevated his tones and even stature, and the man was forgotten in the inspired declaimer.

Our author has a pawky wit, too. "Both these men," he adds unexpectedly, "were living in marital celibacy . . . the lady of each could say of each *His soul is like a star, and dwells apart.*"

VII

But the pages in which our author best convinces and most intrigues me are those of his Seventh Chapter, beginning "It was on the occasion of my returning to my home from Edinburgh, some years since, that I first met the present poet laureate—William Wordsworth. Coming to his little paradise of a mountain domicile, with its amiable inmates, including Miss Wordsworth, a sister of the poet, from the Northern Athens, the literary atmosphere of which is, or was then, above blood-heat, it seemed quite delightful by its serene contrast."

Now when the account of this visit appeared, even in 1847, when the second edition appeared, Wordsworth was still living and in full enjoyment of strong views on capital punishment: and though it is not unknown to me what an interviewer will dare and do in the practise of his craft—in coaxing the unveracious out of the non-existent—I find it hard to believe this particular interview, or series of interviews, to be less than authentic. But here again let me read you a passage or two as exercise in the art of Judging for Yourself, which, whether in Literature or in Science, should be the first aim of a University education.

The business began badly. The guest of the "moderate mansion" and his entertainers were seated at "the delightful tea-table" and "were already deep in the topic of *The Old Thorn*" (of the *Lyrical Ballads*). "Mr. Words-

worth favouring me by relating the precise occasion of
its composition; his being in reality caught in a storm on
a Somersetshire hill: there being an actual lichened
thorn, and also some likeness of a child's grave (which
must be a small green hillock, and therefore might very
well be thought a grave, without allowing for a poet's
or traveller's licence), Mrs. Wordsworth patiently wait-
ing, with hand extended, for the poet's tea-cup, which he
held, but still retained empty as he passed from copious
reminiscence to denounce the laughter at his poetic
theory." At this point it would appear that the guest
incautiously let fall the name of Jeffrey, famous editor
of *The Edinburgh Review.*

"Up started the tall figure of the lyrist, his hitherto
complacent countenance, which was very expressive in
spite of dim eyes and a hard outline, ruffled like his own
little pond that he had 'measured from side to side,' . . .
and with one hand thrust into his breast, and the other
clenched, began a rapid walk around the room, all the
time in good set terms, not rapid like his motions, talking
a review of the *Review,* sometimes of the work *in toto;*
sometimes of its serious onslaught on himself and on his
Excursion, then of Mr. Jeffrey, who 'might think it like
a great man, and worthy of his public character, publicly
to insult another: but *he* also must abide the judgment
of the public,—*slow,* indeed, occasionally, to do justice—
slow,' and he repeated the words, as if pondering, and
becalmed himself with some inward reflection, and then
obeyed Mrs. Wordsworth's anxious invitation to take his
tea before it was quite cold. *'We shall all be judged,'* he
again said energetically; with such solemnity, too, that
it might be thought to allude to doomsday, by anyone
just entering. To allay the storm, his guest recounted
agreeably how he had first, in an odd fashion, made

acquaintance with the *Lyrical Ballads*, picking up a copy (*minus* its title-page) in a road near Epping Forest, where it 'had been dropped, probably, from some vehicle'; and, though at first supposing it to be a book for children, could not help being impressed on perusal by parts of it. Wordsworth was 'much pleased' and, turning to the ladies, pointed out how this accident 'afforded strong evidence in support of his theory, of the latent elements of poetic pleasure even in the lowest walks of life'." "I did not," acknowledges the interviewer, "quite clearly see *how* it bore on the point, but he did; and they, almost before he could end the sentence, were convinced."

I wish I could linger over a drizzling moonlight walk, in the course of which Mr. Wordsworth, after stepping back for his hat and umbrella and quietly bidding his family not to sit up, "began an eloquent discourse on Milton, Dante, himself"—his habits—his literary wrongs again—and a laudatory review in *Blackwood* (by Christopher North). He again evinced his sensitiveness to this laudation in the family circle. "I am told," said he indifferently, "for I have not seen it, that my last publication is reviewed or alluded to; and the extravagant critic goes on to say that the extracts they give are worth, of themselves, the price of the Magazine." This was spoken as a joke, but, it seemed, was not to be so taken: for on his wife's laughing his countenance lowered, "That was a *serious* review, Mrs. Wordsworth."

VIII

Ah, Gentlemen, the egotism of our sex, and its gape for woman's flattery! Here is Wordsworth accurately (I think) depicted: there, away south at Highgate, lingers out Coleridge, on whose long decrepitude it were cruel to descant—and superfluous, since so many have made it their theme. And here at the tea-table sits Dorothy, the good angel of them both—a little old lady in a large be-ribboned cap, her once delicate cheeks bulging a little from a habitual stoop—of lifelong adoration, of lifelong immolation—which shall we say? "It was pleasing," writes our interviewer, "to observe the fond veneration for her brother of the affable and unaffected sister, an ornament of old-maiden life."

O caeca pectora! Blind hearts of mortals, the laurels cut in the woods, the slow surrender, the final acceptance, the bowing of the neck! . . . which, if youth could foresee, youth would surely recoil from, to choose an early death by preference. And in the biographies of obstinate strong-willed men—such as William Wordsworth was—you will usually find that two or three gentler hearts are drained—if not without a thought, yet implacably, to feed the trench around the altar—one friend at least, and at the least a woman or two. I have a thought that Wordsworth, less self-centred, might have saved even Coleridge: we *know* he might have saved an infinity of anguish to Annette Vallon whom he had loved and abandoned in France, and an infinity of patient suffering to his sister Dorothy:

> My sister ('tis a wish of mine),
> Come forth and feel the sun.

Yes, yes!

IX

But let us trace back "the affable and unaffected sister, an ornament of old-maiden life" some forty years or so

to that wonderful summer—that month or two consecrated in our literature—when the Coleridges sojourned
at Nether Stowey and the Wordsworths at Alfoxden in
pleasant Somerset, but a coombe or so dividing them;
where the *Ancient Mariner* was written, the *Lyrical
Ballads* planned, and Dorothy kept her first Journal,

> And at the rainbow's foot lay surely gold
> And hope felt strong, and life itself not weak.

There is trouble, human trouble, on either side of the
dividing glens. Over Nether Stowey reigns a feckless-
ness soon to pass, already passing, to its inevitable sequel
which the feckless, self-deceiving, will of course come
to cover up by the phrase "incompatibility of temper"—
of all human phrases the lowest sneak against lovers'
vows, fair love's loyalty. Across the coombe dwells
Dorothy, too well curing brother William of the last
pangs of his defeasance to honour and a natural tie;
herself at her window, thinking across the starred night
of the other man, the Coleridge she might but for an
accident have saved and lived in his genius a fairy
princess, happy ever after.

But meanwhile we are young, and the gods will somehow, sooner or later, unbend their brows. The two men
have discovered romance as their true ultimate solace.
Pending its efficacy Coleridge drinks laudanum and
Wordsworth the milder and more assimilable bohea of
female adulation. Both are drugs: yes, even the second,
absorbed by a penitent north-countryman and corrected
by punctual out-of-door exercise. And for the while
each finds his drug, operating on strong youth, at once
a narcotic against the gnawing sense of dereliction and
a stimulus to such imaginative effort as never was.

Dorothy keeps a Journal of those days in Somerset: as later, and all the long while that Coleridge is fading out, she keeps one at Grasmere: and later yet of various tours she took with her brother. These Journals, not revealing the inmost heart—or revealing it but now and then, and unintentionally and by glimpses only—seem to me to constitute one of the most pathetic documents in our literature.

X

But let us wipe out all pathos for a moment and consider some few details coldly, almost technically.

While I quote the following entry, you who read and remember your Wordsworth will collate it in your minds with his fairly well-known poem *The Beggars*. The place is Grasmere; the date Tuesday the 10th of June, 1800, but the weather has turned to "a very cold cheerless evening."

A very tall woman, tall much beyond the measure of tall women, called at the door. She had on a very long brown cloak and a very white cap, without bonnet. Her face was excessively brown, but it had plainly once been fair. She had a little bare-footed child about two years old by the hand, and said her husband, who was a tinker, was gone before with the other children. I gave her a piece of bread. Afterwards on my way to Ambleside, beside the bridge at Rydale, I saw her husband sitting by the roadside, his two asses feeding beside him, and the two young children at play upon the grass. The man did not beg. I passed on and about a quarter of a mile further I saw two boys before me, one about 10, the other about 8 years old, at play chasing a butterfly. . . . The hat of the elder was wreathed round with yellow flowers; the younger, whose hat was only a brimless crown, had stuck it round with laurel leaves. They continued to play till I

drew very near, and then they addressed me with the begging
cant and the whining voice of sorrow. I said "I served your
mother this morning" (the boys were so like the woman . . .
that I could not be mistaken). "O!" says the elder, "you could
not serve my mother, for she's dead, and my father's on at
the next town—he's a potter."

I persisted in my assertion, and that I would give them
nothing. Says the elder, "Let's away," and away they flew
like lightning.

Well there, noted in Dorothy's diary, you have an incident—a "thing seen" as the French say—in the course
of a commonplace walk. The diary lies open to brother
William's perusal, and William makes a poem out of it,
a stanza or two of which I must quote for my purpose—

She had a tall man's height or more;
Her face from summer's noontide heat
No bonnet shaded, but she wore
A mantle, to her very feet
Descending *with a graceful flow,*
And on her head a cap as white *as driven snow.* . . .

Advancing, forth she stretch'd her hand
And begged an alms with doleful plea
That ceased not: on our English land
Such woes, I knew, could never be:
And yet a boon I gave her, for the creature
Was beautiful to see—a weed of glorious feature.

I left her, and pursued my way;
And soon before me did espy
A pair of little Boys at play,
Chasing a crimson butterfly;
The taller followed with his hat in hand,
Wreath'd round with yellow flowers, *the gayest of the land.*

The other wore a rimless crown
With leaves of laurel stuck about;
And while both follow'd up and down,
Each whooping with a merry shout,
In their fraternal feature I could trace
Unquestionable lines of that wild Suppliant's face. . . .

They dart across my path—but lo,
Each ready with a plaintive whine!
Said I, "not half an hour ago
Your Mother has had alms of mine."
"That cannot be," one answer'd—"She is dead":
I look'd reproof—they saw—but neither hung his head.

"She has been dead, Sir, many a day."—
"Hush, boys! you're telling me a lie;
It was your Mother, as I say."
And, in the twinkling of an eye,
"Come! Come!" cried one, and without more ado
Off to some other play the joyous Vagrants flew!

XI

Now has Wordsworth—ask yourselves this—*improved* here upon the modest prose entry which he has so obviously copied? Has he made immortal poetry out of prose that scarcely reckoned itself even as prose? Has he not even worsened it with poetical clichés—the beggarwoman's frock "descending with a graceful flow," her cap "as white as driven snow," the boy's wreath of yellow flowers "the gayest of the land"—each dragged in to patch a rhyme? Wordsworth himself was harder than any theoriser upon mere diction. Yet here, if anywhere, we have it lending *in*-verisimilitude to a simple and unpretentious narrative. But wait a moment. I have omitted one stanza about those two urchins—

Yet they, so blithe of heart, seem'd fit
For finest tasks of earth or air:
Wings let them have, and they might flit
Precursors to Aurora's car,
Scattering fresh flowers: though happier far, I ween,
To hunt their fluttering game o'er rock and level green.

That is the lovely thought—that something just beyond her which Dorothy lived to incite. You know how Mrs. Wordsworth, in turn yoked to the service, did her best and once, by a flash, achieved a triumph, announcing that she feels her heart, somehow or other, dancing with the daffodils—a hint which her husband promptly utilised for one of his loveliest lyrics—"I wander'd lonely as a cloud." As for Dorothy's Journals, they teem with hints, phrases, jottings, suggestions, of which her adored brother made use complacently, lordily. It is to me— the whole story as I trace her Journals—curiously reminiscent of the old ache with which one read of Maggie Tulliver and her brother in George Eliot's *The Mill on the Floss.* Sometimes William improves on her, sometimes not. A month after meeting with the Beggars she records—

After tea we rowed down to Loughrigg Fell, visited the white foxglove and walked up to view Rydale. . . .The lake was now most still. . . .We heard a strange sound in the Bainriggs wood, as we were floating on the water: it *seemed* in the wood, but it must have been above it, for presently we saw a raven very high above us. It called out, and *the dome of the sky seemed to echo the sound.*

Turn to your *Excursion,* Bk. IV, and find it transmuted— in a lovely passage—into

> The solitary raven, flying
> Athwart the concave of the dark blue dome,
> Unseen, perchance above all power of sight—
> An iron knell! With echoes from afar
> Faint—and still fainter. . . .

Take *The Leech-Gatherer,* take a dozen other poems.
You will find them all in Dorothy, in parts all but literally
transcribed.

XII

And yet, and always, I find the touch of Coleridge,
operating on some casual passage in these Journals, more
magical, more mysterious. For Wordsworth, although
in many respects classical, had (as you all will admit) his
mannerisms. Or let me put it to you in another way.—
Quite a number of us, presented with a page of Dorothy
and commanded to turn it into half-a-dozen or a dozen
stanzas of typically Wordsworthian verse, might achieve
a passable parody. We should miss, of course, that final
touch which ever and again redeems the great poet. But
Wordsworth himself, even in his best-known poems, did
not always or by any means inevitably achieve that touch.
We could compose, I think, in parody something osten-
sibly his. But who can parody Coleridge as a poet? Let
me suggest to you, for your assent, this criticism of
Francis Thompson's. After quoting a confession by
Coventry Patmore—"I did not try to *imitate* his style.
I can hardly explain *how* he influenced me: he was
rather an ideal of perfect style than a model to imitate:
but in some indescribable way he *did* influence my
development more than any other poet"—Thompson goes
on:

One might as well try to paint air as to catch a style so void of all manner that it is visible, like air, only in its results. All other poets have not only a style, but a manner; not only style, but features of style. The style of Coleridge is bare of manner, without feature, not distinguishable in member, joint, and limb; it is, in the Roman sense of *merum,* mere style; style unalloyed and integral. Imitation has no foothold; it would tread on glass.

I can claim that before ever reading that, I had spoken something to the same effect from this desk. Quoting a stanza or two from *The Ancient Mariner,* such as

> The moving Moon went up the sky,
> And nowhere did abide;
> Softly she was going up,
> And a star or two beside—

"We forget almost," I said, "listening to the voice, that there are such things as words.

> And now 'twas like all instruments,
> Now like a lonely flute;
> And now it is an angel's song,
> That makes the Heavens be mute.

"If in criticism, such an epithet be pardonable, we would call that voice seraphic; if such a simile, we would liken it to a seraph's, musing, talking before the gate of Paradise in the dawn."

XIII

Yes, never was voice than Coleridge's more

> seraphically free
> From taint of personality.

But now take these few scattered sentences from Dorothy's Journals of the Alfoxden days—

Walked from seven o'clock till half past eight. . . . Only once while we were in the wood the moon burst through the invisible veil which enveloped her, the shadows of the oaks blackened, and their lines became more strongly marked. . . . The manufacturer's dog makes a large, uncouth howl, which it continues many minutes after there is no noise near it but that of the brook.

March 7th. William and I drank tea at Coleridge's. A cloudy sky. Observed nothing particularly interesting—the distant prospect obscured. One only leaf upon the top of a tree—the sole remaining leaf—danced round and round like a rag blown by the wind.

March 24th. Coleridge, the Chesters, and Ellen Cruikshank called. We walked with them through the wood. . . . A duller night than last night; a sort of white shade over the blue sky. The stars dim. The spring continues to advance very slowly. . . . The crooked arm of the old oak tree points upwards to the moon.

25th (next evening). Walked to Coleridge's after tea. Arrived at home at one o'clock. The night cloudy but not dark.

Let us put these passages together and behold them transmuted into Coleridge's poetry.

> Sir Leoline, the Baron rich,
> Hath a toothless mastiff bitch;
> From her kennel beneath the rock
> She maketh answer to the clock.
> Four for the quarters, and twelve for the hour;
> Ever and aye, by shine and shower,
> Sixteen short howls, not over loud;
> Some say, she sees my lady's shroud.

Is the night chilly and dark?
The night is chilly, but not dark.
The thin grey cloud is spread on high,
It covers but not hides the sky.
The moon is behind, and at the full;
And yet she looks both small and dull.
The night is chill, the cloud is grey:
'Tis a month before the month of May,
And the Spring comes slowly up this way. . . .

The lady sprang up suddenly,
The lovely lady, Christabel!
It moaned as near, as near can be,
But what it is she cannot tell.—
On the other side it seems to be
Of the huge, broad-breasted, old oak tree.

The night is chill; the forest bare;
Is it the wind that moaneth bleak?
There is not wind enough in the air
To move away the ringlet curl
From the lovely lady's cheek—
There is not wind enough to twirl
The one red leaf, the last of its clan,
That dances as often as dance it can,
Hanging so light, and hanging so high,
On the topmost twig that looks up at the sky.

Now if we come back from technicality and return (as we ever should in considering literature) upon the human heart, I suggest to you a reason on Dorothy's side why, apart from their own contribution to the process, Coleridge rarefies to a degree which William seldom touches—

O Lady, we receive but what we give!

William has left some exquisite poems and passages as tribute to his sister; Coleridge no memorable word on the noble woman who might, but for cross of circumstance, have been his bride and have saved his soul alive. No sisterly devotion, no sisterly tenderness, can match in urgency (it is written by Nature) the "marriage of true minds." It may help, support, console: but it can pass through no alembic in which truly wedded spirits meet to distil a third.

I conclude today, Gentlemen, with two brief extracts from Dorothy's Journals, and shall trust them to you without comment. The first is dated, Grasmere, Sunday 31st of August, 1800.

At 11 o'clock Coleridge came, when I was walking in the still clear moonshine in the garden. He came over Helvellyn. William was gone to bed. . . . We sate and chatted till half-past three . . . Coleridge reading a part of *Christabel*.

Here is the second—Coleridge away and derelict by now—

Monday, 8th February, 1802. After dinner (i.e. we set off at about half-past four) we went towards Rydale for letters. . . . The rain had been so cold that it hardly melted the snow. We stopped at Park's to get some straw for W'm's shoes. . . . Before we had come to the shore of the lake we met our patient bow-bent friend, with his little wooden box on his back. "Where are you going?" said he. "To Rydale for letters." " I have two for you in my box." We lifted up the lid, and there they lay. . . . We broke the seal of Coleridge's letter, and I had light enough to see that he was not ill. I put it in my pocket. At the top of the White Moss I took it to my bosom—a safer place for it. . . . N.B. The moon came out suddenly . . . and a star or two beside.

DOROTHY WORDSWORTH (II)

I

IN Plato's *Menexenus* you will find attributed to
Aspasia, that wonderful mistress of Pericles, a funeral
oration over the Athenian dead who had recently fallen
in battle. It is fine in its fashion though not comparable,
of course, with the triumphant speech—possession for all
for ever—which Thucydides reports for us. In the
First Book of Livy we are told how Numa, second and
gentle patriarch king, building Rome, learnt his wisdom
from Egeria, virgin goddess of well-springs, communing
with her in holy groves. I think, Gentlemen, that some-
one is wanted to clutch these and many other womanly
shadows out of oblivion—shades of women who have
made great men. In our *Dictionary of National Biography,* admittedly a comprehensive work, you will find
no word on Dorothy Wordsworth—the spirit that, subservient always as an Ariel, took and shaped Wordsworth and Coleridge, made them what the one became,
what the other so gloriously was for a while, and then—
was not.

II

In my previous lecture I spoke at some length of her
influence on Coleridge, intending to deal today with what
she did for her brother, and, through him, for English

poetry. Well, as I was counting up the sum of his debt
to her and in the very act of wondering at it, there came
to me—quite unawares, and just as things *do* happen in
this queer world—tidings of a book about Dorothy by
Miss Catherine Maclean, of the University College of
Cardiff. My nescience of it had even the less claim on
pardon because our own University Press had printed
and reprinted it (as it deserved) within the last year.
But never let us mind little things like that, Gentlemen;
the great thing is that the good people should sooner or
later come to their own and their virtue to survive in us.
As Jane Austen makes Miss Bates observe "And they
always do, you know." Yes; and even on the 16th of
last month I opened my *Times Literary Supplement*
upon a letter of Professor Sélincourt, asking for any
fugitive memorials available of this Dorothy. So permanent may be the worth, so persistent the effect of a
good thing in this transitory world, that somehow or
other, and apparently quite at hazard, there gathers
among people who have never even met one another a
common instinct to redeem some precious jewel, and
remind the world of its true value—although, to be sure,
the image of Dorothy has never lacked lustre for true
students of the Lake poets and their place in the
Romantic Revival.

III

And so it just happened that some twelve or fourteen
days ago, I picked up Miss Maclean's book and lit upon
a paragraph almost exactly expressing what I intended to
write (if I could have attained to saying it so well) as a
prelude to today's enquiry. Therefore in the interests of
economy I shall quote it unabashed—

Dorothy gave Wordsworth a great deal. She gave him all she had to give except her quick sense of humour. Yet, as we read her journals, our wonder is, not that he took so much, but that he did not take more. They are so rich in the rough material of poetry. Much of them consists of poetry unwrought into verse.

—On which I pause for a moment to comment that the shield of Achilles itself is mighty fine in conception and suggestion until Hephaistos, the workman, scratches his head and does it—

One thing is worth noticing, that as Wordsworth's faculty decayed, he ceased to receive inspiration from Dorothy, who retained her powers as long as she wrote. . . To suggest that Wordsworth was guilty of anything like plagiarism is nonsense. His specific gift is quite different from Dorothy's. She is made no whit the poorer by her brother's gain and by the suggestions he caught from her richness. The fact was, these two had the knack of setting each other on fire. If any criticism is to be made on Wordsworth's use of Dorothy's material it is that he did not seem to realise the beauty of that on which he drew . . . that the material he was borrowing from Dorothy and fashioning into new shapes was already gold. With this obtuseness of his with regard to a poetic inspiration more constant than his own, it is impossible—says Miss Maclean—not to feel the utmost impatience. There is only one excuse for him. Dorothy's extraordinary modesty might have misled even a surer critic than William Wordsworth.

Now with the conclusion of the above passage I find myself unable to agree. It certainly does Wordsworth less than justice, and, to my thinking, does him no little positive injustice. With the writer's fervour in championing Dorothy (as you must know, who did me the

honour of listening to a previous lecture) I go all the
way; she has my full sympathy with her zeal to restore
this wonderful woman, inspiring handmaid of some of
the greatest poetry in our language—friend, too, of
Hazlitt, of De Quincey, and of Charles Lamb a very
dear friend—to her just rights. But I somewhat suspect
the petulance of the last sentences quoted to be just a
little unhistorical; that is to say, that it arises from the
impatience of a young woman of the present day, having
privileges, with the treatment of her sex in the past:
and, if I be right, I suggest that it should have been
directed rather against the social era in which the
Wordsworths lived than against Wordsworth himself.
After all, one may say in parenthesis that there were
few women poets in that era, and none of them very
good—at any rate unless you count Joanna Baillie and
Mrs. Barbauld—none certainly to compare with such
men as Cowper, Burns, Blake, Coleridge, Wordsworth
himself, Shelley, Keats, Byron. Poetry, I fear, was not
definitely recognized as woman's business, and Dorothy
—most modest of women—never assumed that it was.
De Quincey, for instance, is blamed because after a visit
to Grasmere, in describing the person and characteristics
of Dorothy, he concludes with the words—"To talk of
her 'writings' is too pompous an expression, or at least
far beyond any pretensions that she ever made for
herself."

Also, be it remembered, the Wordsworths lived rus-
tically and came of country stock: and it is not of Comedy
alone that we can say, with Meredith, that it flourishes
only when women are on the road to an equal footing
with men in attainments and liberty. We can say of
literature in general that only when women are on the
road to an equal footing with men and only enjoy an

equal liberty, they have anything like an equal chance. But to speak individually of Wordsworth, let us remember that he was a Dalesman and, while adoring his womankind, accepted their services with the equanimity born of the ingrained prejudice of a Dalesman.

IV

But that Wordsworth fully realized his debt to his sister is evident on page after page of his poetry. That he loved her, everybody knows. "In boyhood," writes Dorothy, "he was never afraid of comforting his sister; he never left her in anger; he always met her with joy; he preferred her society to every other pleasure—or, rather, when we were so happy as to be within each other's reach, he had no pleasure when we were compelled to be divided." And William writes, "How much do I wish that each emotion of pleasure or pain within me, by that sympathy which will almost identify us when we have stolen into our little cottage . . . I will write to my uncle, and tell him I cannot think of going anywhere before I have been with you. Whatever answer he gives me, I certainly will make a point of once more mingling my transports with yours. Alas! my dear sister, how soon must this happiness expire; yet there are moments worth ages." Again he says, "Oh, my dear, dear sister, with what transport shall I again meet you! with what rapture shall I again wear out the day in your sight! . . . I see you in a moment running, or rather flying to my arms."

But now let us turn to the poems and, merely by way of illustrations, select two pairs of passages and see how in each pair Wordsworth passes from confessing affection to admitting his intellectual debt to his sister.

In the year 1798 he indites his lyrical invitation *To My Sister*:—

It is the first mild day of March:
Each minute sweeter than before,
The redbreast sings from the tall larch
That stands beside our door.

There is a blessing in the air,
Which seems a sense of joy to yield
To the bare trees, and mountains bare,
And grass in the green field.

My sister! ('tis a wish of mine)
Now that our morning meal is done,
Make haste, your morning task resign;
Come forth and feel the sun.

No joyless forms shall regulate
Our living calendar:
We from to-day, my Friend, will date
The opening of the year.

Love, now a universal birth,
From heart to heart is stealing,
From earth to man, from man to earth:
—It is the hour of feeling.

One moment now may give us more
Than years of toiling reason:
Our minds shall drink at every pore
The spirit of the season.

A quatrain which, later in the same year, he converted into these immortal lines—

One impulse from a vernal wood
May teach you more of man,
Of moral evil and of good,
Than all the sages can.

Let us continue—

And from the blessed power that rolls
About, below, above,
We'll frame the measure of our souls:
They shall be tuned to love.

Then come, my Sister! come, I pray,
With speed put on your woodland dress;
And bring no book: for this one day
We'll give to idleness.

Thus far we have indeed the underlying sense of a twin communion with Nature; but, beyond that, little more than brotherly love. But now turn to that famous lyric, written in 1801 :—

The Sparrow's Nest

Behold, within the leafy shade,
Those bright blue eggs together laid!
On me the chance-discovered sight
Gleamed like a vision of delight.
I started—seeming to espy
The home and sheltered bed,
The Sparrow's dwelling, which, hard by
My Father's house, in wet or dry
My sister Emmeline and I
   Together visited.

She looked at it and seemed to fear it;
Dreading, tho' wishing, to be near it:

Such heart was in her, being then
A little Prattler among men.
The Blessing of my later years
Was with me when a boy:
She gave me eyes, she gave me ears;
And humble cares, and delicate fears:
A heart, the fountain of sweet tears;
   And love, and thought, and joy.

"She gave me eyes, she gave me ears." . . . Is that not a confession?

Now for my second pair of quotations, both from *The Prelude*. The first is from a passage describing a vacation holiday from Cambridge:

Above all joys, that seemed another morn
Risen on mid noon; blest with the presence, Friend,
Of that sole Sister, her who hath been long
Dear to thee also, thy true friend and mine,
Now, after separation desolate,
Restored to me—such absence that she seemed
A gift then first bestowed. The varied banks
Of Emont, hitherto unnamed in song,

    .   .   .   .   .   .

Have seen us side by side, when, having clomb
The darksome windings of a broken stair,
And crept along a ridge of fractured wall,
Not without trembling, we in safety looked
Forth, through some Gothic window's open space,
And gathered with one mind a rich reward
From the far-stretching landscape, by the light
Of morning beautified, or purple eve;
Or, not less pleased, lay on some turret's head,
Catching from tufts of grass and hare-bell flowers
Their faintest whisper to the passing breeze,
Given out while mid-day heat oppressed the plains.

Now, before we come to the passage that I would couple with this, let me quote a few words of Earl Grey's, from his *Fallodon Papers:*—

. . . Wordsworth, too, is strong. If he expresses, as he sometimes does, great dejection, great depression, he never rests or brings his poem to an end till he stands with both feet planted on firm ground by some thought which has pulled him up, rescued him from depression, and made him erect and confident. It is interesting to compare Wordsworth and Shelley in this respect. It does not add to the pleasure of reading to exalt one author at the expense of another, and I am not introducing this comparison for the purpose of depreciating Shelley, but you will notice that Shelley is sometimes content to leave you with a cry of despair. Wordsworth, after expressing deep dejection, never ends till he has become confident and strong again. You will find instances of what I mean in Wordsworth's *Lines on the Death of Fox;* you will find it in *The Leech Gatherer,* and you will find it in the *Afterthought* (of the Duddon sonnets), and in many other places.

Very well, I say. But who did this? It was Dorothy. When, in 1792, Wordsworth returned out of France with all his young hopes of the French Revolution laid in the dust, and, upon that, the torturing sense that he had loved there, and defaulted, and betrayed, most naturally he was sunk—as a young man well might be —in depression and almost in despair. He tried to drug his conscience by engaging his mind in the abstract sciences, but these were of no avail. It was at this crisis that, as her nephew, the Bishop of Lincoln, afterwards recorded, Dorothy came to him and weaned and won him back to beauty and truth. William's visits to her had of late been scanty and brief, until the brightening fortune of a legacy allowed them to share a cottage as they had long ago desired to do, and there, in their long walks together, she gradually withdrew him from all worries over political or theoretical puzzles and convinced him that he was born to be a *poet*. And now let us turn to the passage I have in mind, with its double confession:

> Depressed, bewildered thus, I did not walk
> With scoffers, seeking light and gay revenge
> With indiscriminate laughter, nor sate down
> In reconcilement with an utter waste
> Of intellect.
>
> .   .   .   .
>
>   Then it was—
> Thanks to the bounteous Giver of all good!—
> That the beloved sister in whose sight
> Those days were passed, now speaking in a voice
> Of sudden admonition—like a brook
> That did but *cross* a lonely road, and now
> Is seen, heard, felt, and caught at every turn,
> Companion never lost through many a league—
> Maintain'd for me a saving intercourse
> With my true self; for, though bedimmed and changed
> Much, as it seemed, I was no further changed
> Than as a clouded and a waning moon:
> She whispered still that brightness would return;
> *She, in the midst of all, preserved me still*
> *A Poet; made me seek beneath that name,*
> *And that alone, my office upon earth.*

Yes, yes!

       Or like two birds, companions in mid-air,

or again

Or glancing at each other cheerful looks,
Like separated clouds with stars between.

V

But before we go on to discuss, or rather indicate,
details of Dorothy's influence on William, let me break
off to say a word or two upon her story and upon
some records that he and their contemporaries have left
of her appearance and ways. Their parents died when
they were young. Their excellent mother died in 1778
when Dorothy was little more than six years old. After
this loss her father's health declined and, by consequence
of a night of exposure on the moors, he succumbed.
Dorothy, thus left an orphan at the early age of twelve,
was separated now from her brother. William went
to school at Hawkshead, in north Lancashire, when in
his ninth year : and the experiences of his schooldays
are preserved to us in *The Prelude*. Dorothy was com-
mended to the care of uncongenial relatives, and, save
for occasional glimpses of William in the holidays, her
life for the next ten years does not seem to have been a
happy one. Gradually, however, Fate broke the clouds
it had hung between their two lives; first by the happy
period of William's summer vacations from Cambridge,
afterwards by the aid of a small legacy which enabled
them to realise the dream of childhood and set up house
together in a humble cottage. Then followed Wordsworth's disastrous visit to France, and his return to be
nursed back (as we have seen) to cheerfulness and
sanity. Next comes the discovery of Coleridge, the
residence in Somerset, Coleridge at Nether Stowey, the
Wordsworths at Alfoxden, with but a combe dividing
them. And so we arrive at those glorious months of a

glorious summer and of glorious inspiration, the triumph of which may be summarized on the evening of March 23rd, when Dorothy writes in her journal, "Coleridge dined with us. He brought his ballad [*The Ancient Mariner*] finished. We walked with him to the miner's house. A beautiful evening, very starry, the horned moon."

> Till clomb above the Eastern bar
> The horned moon. . . .

—her heart, we perceive, echoing the poem as she had gazed, and still echoing it as she writes. We feel also that the stars were out with excuse, to celebrate the birth of a brother; or perchance to say farewell to him, as he dropped to be held between human hands. There follows later, amid some longings for things which could never be, much domestic felicity, many happy jaunts, the first real tragedy of Dorothy's life, concealing itself under the mask of happiness, and accepted by her under a mask of beautiful resignation so long to be worn that in the end it added another and a habitual charm to her features. I mean, of course, William's marriage to their common friend, Mary Hutchinson. I shall say no more here of Mrs. Wordsworth than that, by all consent, she, "a perfect woman, nobly planned," deserved through life all the encomiums that have been left of her by her husband and by every friend or acquaintance who ever visited either Grasmere or Rydal Mount. The married pair, as we know, took Dorothy to their hearth and home, and she (as we also know) nobly repaid them. For it was she who, when the children came, most anxiously cared for them. If you would divine how tender that care was, turn to her poem *The Mother's Return,* which William, with acknowledgment, included among his own—as well he might, since it was quite in his own manner. It was to Dorothy, let us note, that the whole party invariably resorted for small practical help; whether, on a journey, to see the horse baited, or, at home, to walk into the town and do the necessary shopping.

Over her second tragedy, long drawn out, let me draw the swiftest veil. You may perhaps best gather it for yourselves from the Diaries of Henry Crabb Robinson, and from his *Correspondence with the Wordsworth Circle,* recently edited by Dr. Edith J. Morley. Her mind failed: despite many flashes of recovery, which gave the family hope, she declined slowly—very slowly —and alas! outlived her brother, a Laureate whose own intellectual powers had evaporated. Not for her was the wish realized which he had once expressed in his lines *To a Young Lady, who had been reproached for taking Long Walks in the Country*—

> Thy thoughts and feelings shall not die,
> Nor leave thee, when grey hairs are nigh,
>   A melancholy slave;
> But an old age serene and bright,
> And lovely as a Lapland night,
>   Shall lead thee to thy grave.

VI

And now let us see, as well as we may, the earthly semblance taken by this wonderful creature. She was short of stature, of complexion a deep brown, with wild darting eyes, that saw everything, and a speech so eager to express what she saw and thought that the words between her lips broke into a stammer. First, however, let us take her brother's hints of her appearance and charm. It is well established that the poems addressed

"To Lucy"—that carcanet of lyrics, so charged with love, so chastened of amativeness—written by Wordsworth when abroad, were really intended for Dorothy. You all know the stanzas:

> She shall be sportive as the fawn
> That wild with glee across the lawn
>   Or up the mountain springs;
> And hers shall be the breathing balm,
> And hers the silence and the calm
>   Of mute insensate things.
>
> .   .   .   .
>
> The stars of midnight shall be dear
> To her; and she shall lean her ear
>   In many a secret place
> Where rivulets dance their wayward round,
> And beauty born of murmuring sound
>   Shall pass into her face.

"Wild" is ever the word for her. In *Tintern Abbey* you will note

>   the shooting lights
>   Of thy wild eyes.

Now listen to Coleridge. Writing from Nether Stowey, he says:

Wordsworth and his exquisite sister are with me. She is a woman, indeed!—in mind, I mean, and heart; for her person is such that, if you expected to see a pretty woman, you would think her ordinary; if you expected to see an ordinary woman, you would think her pretty; but her manners are simple, ardent, impressive. In every motion her most innocent soul outbeams so brightly that who saw her would say:

Guilt was a thing impossible in her.

Her information various; her eye watchful in minutest observation of Nature; and her taste a perfect electrometer. It bends, protrudes, and draws in at subtlest beauties and most recondite faults.

De Quincey, as might be expected, is more elaborate:

Immediately behind her (Mrs. Wordsworth) moved a lady shorter, slighter, and perhaps in all other respects as different from her in personal characteristics, as could have been wished for the most effective contrast. Her face was of Egyptian brown; rarely in a woman of English birth had I seen a more determinate Gipsy tan. Her eyes were not soft, as Mrs. Wordsworth's, nor were they fierce or bold; but they were wild and startling, and hurried in their motion. Her manner was warm, and even ardent; her sensibility seemed constitutionally deep; and some subtle fire of impassioned intellect apparently burned within her, which, being alternately pushed forward into a conspicuous expression, by the irrepressible instincts of her temperament, and then immediately checked, in obedience to the decorum of her sex and age, and her maidenly condition, gave to her whole demeanour, and to her conversation, an air of embarrassment, and even of self-conflict, that was almost distressing to witness. Even her very utterance and enunciation often suffered in point of clearness and steadiness from the agitation of her excessive organic sensibility. At times the self-counteraction and self-baffling of her feelings caused her even to stammer, and so determinately to stammer that a stranger who should have seen her and quitted her in that state of feeling, would certainly have set her down for one plagued with that infirmity of speech as distressingly as Charles Lamb himself. This was Miss Wordsworth, the only sister of the poet—his "Dorothy," who naturally owed so much to the lifelong intercourse with her great brother, in his most solitary and sequestered years; but, on the other hand, to whom he has acknowledged obligations of the profoundest nature; and, in particular, this mighty one, through which we also, the admirers and worshippers of this great poet, are become equally her debtors—that whereas the intellect of Wordsworth was, by its original tendency, too stern, too austere, too much enamoured of an ascetic harsh sublimity, she it was—the lady who paced by his side continually through sylvan and mountain tracts—in Highland glens and in the dim recesses of German charcoal burners—that first *couched* his eye to the sense of beauty, humanised him by the gentler charities, and engrafted with her delicate female touch those graces upon the ruder growths of his nature, which have since clothed the forest of his genius with a foliage corresponding in loveliness and beauty to the strength of its boughs and the massiness of its trunks.

Hazlitt found her "incomparable." Charles Lamb does not, so far as I remember, actually describe her. But anybody who knows the art of fiction knows that a detailed inventory is the most primitive of all ways of conveying an impression concerning any person; that the impression can be far more accurately and subtly produced by the record of a gesture or a tone in the conversation. The following letter of Lamb's to Dorothy will perhaps tell you what I mean. It could only have been addressed to a highly intelligent woman by a thoroughly intelligent and affectionate friend. It carries to her a report concerning Wordsworth's small boy "Willy," who had been left, on a visit to London, in charge of the Lambs.

25th November, 1819

Dear Miss Wordsworth,

You will think me negligent: but I wanted to see more of Willy before I ventured to express a prediction. Till yesterday I had barely seen him—Virgilium tantum vidi,—but yesterday he gave us his small company to a bullock's heart, and I can pronounce him a lad of promise. He is no pedant, nor bookworm; so far I can answer. Perhaps he has hitherto paid too little attention to other men's inventions, preferring, like Lord Foppington, the "natural sprouts of his own." But he has observation, and seems thoroughly awake. I am ill at remembering other people's *bon mots,* but the following are a few:—Being taken over Waterloo Bridge, he remarked that if we had no mountains, we had a fine river at least; which was a touch of the comparative: but then he added, in a strain which augured less for his future abilities as a political economist, that he had supposed they must take at least a pound a week toll. Like a curious naturalist, he inquired if the tide did not come up a little salty. This being satisfactorily answered, he put another question, as to the flux and reflux; which being rather cunningly evaded than artfully solved by that she-Aristotle, Mary,—who muttered something about its getting up an hour sooner and sooner every day,—he sagely replied, "Then it must come to the same thing at last"; which was a speech worthy of an infant Halley! The lion in the 'Change by no means came up to his ideal standard, so impossible is it for Nature, in any of her works, to come up to the standard of a child's imagination! The whelps (lionets) he was sorry to find were dead; and, on particular inquiry, his old friend the ourang-outang had gone the way of all flesh also. The grand tiger was also sick, and expected in no short time to exchange this transitory world for another,—or none. But again, there was a golden eagle (I do not mean that of Charing) which did much arride and console him. William's genius, I take it, leans a little to the figurative; for being at play at tricktrack (a kind of minor billiard-table which we keep for smaller wights, and sometimes refresh our own mature fatigues with taking a hand at), not being able to hit a ball he had iterate aimed at, he cried out, "I cannot hit that beast."

Now the balls are usually called men, but he felicitously hit upon a middle term; a term of approximation and imaginative reconciliation; a something where the two ends of the brute matter (ivory), and their human and rather violent personification into men, might meet, as I take it: illustrative of that excellent remark, in a certain preface about imagination, explaining "Like a sea-beast that had crawled forth to sun himself"! Not that I accuse William Minor of hereditary plagiary, or conceive the image to have come *ex traduce*. Rather he seemeth to keep aloof from any source of imitation, and purposely to remain ignorant of what mighty poets have done in this kind before him; for, being asked if his father had ever been on Westminster Bridge, he answered that he did not know!

VII

But before I speak particularly of his sister's influence upon Wordsworth, let me caution you that to dogmatize upon one human being's influence over another is always hazardous unless (1) we have the open admission, of one party or the other (such open admission, e.g., as Plato makes, or Marcus Aurelius), or (2) we can deduce it by chronology (as that Horace and Milton both influenced Cowper) or plain evidence (as that, in the early brief Alfoxden days, Coleridge's mind influenced Wordsworth more than Wordsworth's influenced Coleridge's, until the distraught one became resolute and the positive teacher faded into irresolution). As between Coleridge and Wordsworth it works out to a question of *stamina*.

But when a brother and a sister have been inseparables in childhood and whenever occasion and grown youth permitted, so with regard to some affinities of thought and diction as William and Dorothy exhibit the question at once arises, "May not any resemblance in thought and diction here and there (and there are hundreds, if we search) come from two individual shoots of the same parent stock and sap?"   To put it positively—if, after some years' assaying of the characters and shades of character, I may bring to you my testimony for what you may think it worth, these two Wordsworths had a way of their own, such as you may discover for yourselves if, page by page, you will read William's tract on *The Convention of Cintra* or a *Preface to the Lyrical Ballads* alongside Dorothy's *Journals*.   Again and again this indefinable Wordsworthian way of saying things will, out of a passage of easy limpid prose, flash on your eyes as if out of a conjuror's box.   I have no time today to give you more than one illustrative comparison.   In the famous *Preface* Wordsworth writes—just says—

In spite of differences of soil and climate, of language and manners, of laws and customs; *in spite of things silently gone out of mind, and things violently destroyed;* the Poet binds together by passion and knowledge the vast empire of human society as it is spread over the whole earth, and over all time.

Here is transcendentalism, or whatever you choose to call it.   Now turn back to earth and read a simple passage of how Dorothy and her brother met a poor beggar woman on the banks of Loch Lomond:

Came to a bark hut by the shores, and sate for some time under the shelter of it.   While we were here a poor woman with a little child by her side begged a penny of me, and asked where she could "find quarters in the village."   She was a travelling beggar, a native of Scotland, had often "heard of that water," but was never there before.   This woman's appearance, while the wind was rustling about us, and the waves breaking at our feet, was very melancholy: the waters looked wide, the hills many, and dark, and far off—no house but at Luss. I thought what a dreary waste must this lake be to such poor creatures, *struggling with fatigue and poverty and unknown ways!*

"In spite of things silently gone out of mind, and things violently destroyed"—listen to the overtone:

> Perhaps the plaintive numbers flow
> For old unhappy far-off things
> And battles long ago;

Dorothy heard that

struggling with fatigue and poverty *and unknown ways.*

Chase the undertones of *that* for yourselves through the Poems. "What, are you stepping Westward?"— Dorothy heard *that. The Redbreast chasing the Butterfly,* do you chase *that,* through several poems.

> Oh! pleasant, pleasant were the days,
> The time, when, in our childish plays,
> My sister Emmeline and I
> Together chased the butterfly!
> A very hunter did I rush
> Upon the prey:—with leaps and springs
> I followed on from brake to bush;
> But she, God love her, feared to brush
> The dust from off its wings.

And there, God love her, is Dorothy again; and so on, and so on.

VIII

As I see it, for those of you who have imagination, the whole secret can be read by your studying two passages which I shall now place side by side before you. The first is an extract from Dorothy's *Journals,* just a note of an afternoon's companionship.

I went and sate with William and walked backwards and forwards in the orchard till dinner-time. He read me his poem. I read to him, and my Beloved slept. A sweet evening as it had been a sweet day, and I walked quietly along the side of Rydale lake with quiet thoughts—the hills and the lake were still—the owls had not begun to hoot, and the little birds had given over singing. I looked before me and saw a red light upon Silver How as if coming out of the vale below,

> There was a light of most strange birth,
> A light that came out of the earth,
> And spread along the dark hill-side.

Thus I was going on when I saw the shape of my Beloved in the road at a little distance. We turned back to see the light: but it was fading—almost gone.

And now for a pendant, those famous lines from *Tintern Abbey*:

>   Nor perchance,
> If I were not thus taught, should I the more
> Suffer my genial spirits to decay:
> For thou art with me here upon the banks
> Of this fair river; thou my dearest Friend,
> My dear, dear Friend; and in thy voice I catch
> The language of my former heart, and read
> My former pleasures in the shooting lights

Of thy wild eyes. Oh! yet a little while
May I behold in thee what I was once,
My dear, dear Sister! and this prayer I make,
Knowing that Nature never did betray
The heart that loved her; 'tis her privilege,
Through all the years of this our life, to lead
From joy to joy; for she can so inform
The mind that is within us, so impress
With quietness and beauty, and so feed
With lofty thoughts, that neither evil tongues,
Rash judgments, nor the sneers of selfish men,
Nor greetings where no kindness is, nor all
The dreary intercourse of daily life,
Shall e'er prevail against us, or disturb
Our cheerful faith, that all which we behold
Is full of blessings. Therefore let the moon
Shine on thee in thy solitary walk;
And let the misty mountain-winds be free
To blow against thee: and, in after years,
When these wild ecstasies shall be matured
Into a sober pleasure; when thy mind
Shall be a mansion for all lovely forms,
Thy memory be as a dwelling-place
For all sweet sounds and harmonies; oh! then,
If solitude, or fear, or pain, or grief,
Should be thy portion, with what healing thoughts
Of tender joy wilt thou remember me,
And these my exhortations! Nor perchance—
If I should be where I no more can hear
Thy voice, nor catch from thy wild eyes these gleams
Of past existence—wilt thou then forget
That on the banks of this delightful stream
We stood together; and that I, so long
A worshipper of Nature, hither came
Unwearied in that service: rather say
With warmer love—oh! with far deeper zeal

Of holier love. Nor wilt thou then forget,
That after many wanderings, many years
Of absence, these steep woods and lofty cliffs,
And this green pastoral landscape, were to me
More dear, both for themselves and for thy sake!

IX

I shall conclude, Gentlemen, by saying a yet bolder thing. I suppose we may all agree that the Romantic Movement, as it is called, was, at any rate to a great extent, a revolt of the individual spirit against a false tradition which taught that the test of high poetry lay in the poet's power to *generalize* magnificently, or at any rate impressively. Listen, for example, to Dr. Johnson in his *Life of Cowley*—

Sublimity is produced by aggregation, and littleness by dispersion. Great thoughts are always general, and consist in positions not limited by exceptions, and in descriptions not descending to minuteness;

to which Blake, in a scribbled note on a margin to Sir Joshua Reynolds's *Discourses,* makes bold answer:

To generalize is to be an idiot. To particularize is the great distinction of merit.

That is all very well. I suppose there is no one in this room who regrets that there was ever such a thing as the Romantic Revival: and I am well aware that if I attempted here to say a word against Blake (whom I worship) or against Burns (whom I worship, and, I really do think, a little more intelligently than the mass of his countrymen), I should have taken the precaution to have an escort ready on horseback by the postern gate, or at any rate to run for my life.

But Blake, after all, was a Londoner and wove his wonderful imaginings out of himself, with very little detailed knowledge or understanding of "England's green and pleasant land"; while, as for Burns, as a ploughman he took his natural surroundings for granted, and a daisy or a field-mouse were to him but incitements to sentimentalizing. It is in *Mary Morison* or in "My luv's like a red, red rose" (that is to say, in lyrics wonderfully adapted out of old folk-songs) that Burns breathes Scotland at his best. But *porro unum est necessarium.* In spite of what James Thomson had done in *The Seasons* and Dr. Darwin was feeling for in *The Botanic Garden,* the Romantics yet lacked that piercing eye for Nature, in the full Greek sense of the term, which could link up her secrets with high philosophical generalizations such as are to be found in Wordsworth's *Tintern Abbey.* It was the Wordsworths, brother and sister, who discovered this secret. They needed not, as the later flamboyant Romantics needed, the very Alps on which to discharge their violent emotions, on which of their own accord to nail their bodies for a prey to vultures of their own inviting. The Wordsworths took our homely England, in wilder or gentler aspect. They walked the mountains; yet, coming home they knew the homely truth that

> To your orchard hedge belong
> All the pomp and plume of song.

And it was Dorothy, who missed no flower or bird, or comparison of moonlight or sunlight, that unloosed the tied spirit of her brother. From boyhood, indeed, the sounding cataract had haunted him like a passion; but until she taught him the meaning of it had remained inexpressible. She touched his lips; and, through him, she has left her benign influence upon all later Romantic poets, to this day.

She gave them eyes, she gave them ears.

SHAKESPEARE'S COMEDIES

A LECTURE on this subject (chosen for me) must needs, at the outset, be suspected of promising flimsiness, superficiality. To speak generally, at this time of day, of the genius of Shakespeare is, according as you take it, either absurdly easy or supremely difficult. To expatiate upon Shakespeare at this time of day is "a career open to all the talents"; to speak particularly of recent discoveries (or supposed discoveries) about the First Folio and relative value of the Quartos might soon weary. To tell you anything at once generally true and new enough to be useful is a task equally difficult and dangerous. Nevertheless, let us invoke the gods.

I

I have engaged myself to speak of Shakespeare's Comedies; and I begin by asking you to run your minds over them (fourteen in the Canon) and ask yourselves if they be not, in your minds, something *sui generis*. You may, or may not, have reached beyond a vague notion of this, with a sense of the man's transcendency, maybe a little obscured by Lamb's or Swinburne's too indiscriminate worship of Elizabethan dramatists good, bad and indifferent. But I suggest the very vagueness of that notion may give us a useful start. It will at once rid our discussion of hampering *à priori* definitions of what "Comedy" is and what a Comedy ought to be; framed by Critics who were never at the expense of writing one. Shakespeare wrote entrancing plays, which Heminge and Condell in the First Folio of 1623 divided (with some evidence of a halting conviction when they came to *Troilus and Cressida*) into Mr. William Shakespeare's Comedies, Histories and Tragedies. The first of these divisions concerns us this evening, and the question, has it a *suum genus?*—a difference of its own—separating it from the Comedies written by other men before and after him, in this Country and in various others?

II

It may seem to invite disaster that a lecturer asks you thus early to half-close your eyes and even your ears. But I do. I ask you to close eyes and ears half-way for a moment and retire your minds into your own memories and general concept of a Comedy by William Shakespeare—a sort of composite photograph. I don't care how it works out, or what comes first, what uppermost. It may mix up verse lovely and memorable with lewd back-chat of servants and chop-logic of clowns and courtiers; you may throw in the flowers dropped from Dis's wagon with the tavern-score found in Falstaff's pocket; Puck and Ariel with Shylock and Abhorson; you may mix up Dogberry, Sly, Jaques, Holofernes with the scenery and music amid which they move. So, surrendering yourself to these undertones, you may go even drowsily down the gallery of his good maidens— Sylvia, Portia, Sweet Anne Page, Rosalind, Celia, Viola, Perdita, Miranda—their very names linked in carillon, chiming down from this man's celestial belfry.

III

Well, now, after some such surrender to the general impression of memory, we shall awake (no matter which detail lasts uppermost) to a sense that somehow, and apart from any mere theatrical skill, Shakespeare's Comedies are things of themselves, and from that begin to work out their essential difference upon a process of *Exclusion*.

IV

To start with, we find ourselves miles away from any definition of Comedy save that a "Comic" play has a happy ending. But *Cymbeline, a Tragedy* has a complete happy ending, whereas *A Winter's Tale,* labelled "a Comedy," runs on straight lines of tragedy for almost half its length, is switched off into Sicilian or Bohemian pastoral and ends in what Aristotle would have roundly called melodrama: each of these plays depending on "poetic justice" in the end—that is on an apportionment of awards among the sheep and the goats.

Or again, how can you call (under any ordinary definition) *Measure for Measure* a Comedy, running as it does all alongside the pit of hell and only redeemed to health by a posturer and a dirty trick contrived under a sense of chastity utterly false and warped to us, even as the conclusion of *All's Well* is warped? I instance these plays merely as warning-posts to us not to use any pre-conceived definition of Comedy upon the Shakesperian Canon.

V

To proceed, then, on our line of exclusion.—If we open our eyes to focus them upon any chosen Comedy

of Shakespeare's, we see at once that it differs in notion
from any "Citizen Comedy," whether written by Ben
Jonson, Heywood, or Dekker in their several veins.
Shakespeare knew his Eastcheap right enough, with its
denizens, down to Pistol and Doll Tearsheet. Yet, including (as we must in our survey) these Falstaffian
scenes and persons, we perceive that they differ by intention and dramatic purpose from the jolly vulgarities
of Dekker's *Shoemaker's Holiday* as from Jonson's
Londoners and the brothels and gutters into which he
deliberately plunged his learned Plautine sock. For one
difference, these Citizen plays have their main concern
with *bourgeois* plots, *bourgeois* happenings; in this following, as we shall see, a dictum of Castelvetro's, that
Comedy, being entirely concerned with the ludicrous,
uses only such characters as are of poor spirit and mean
estate : whereas Shakespeare is habitually for the Court,
for grandees. *Their* fortunes make his main theme.
Even when, by Royal command, he has to write a play
all about Falstaff, he sets it among decent folk in and
around Windsor Park, with the Castle for background.
Usually when the toe of his low comedian (peasant or
Cockney) has to gall the kibe of his courtier, he just
lets it wander in, whether to supply satirical comment or
the relief of blunt fooling. Over this art of interruption
(as I will call it) he has such assurance of mastery that
he dares to use it, to poke fun at it, even in *Hamlet,* in
the Gravediggers' Scene. In the Comedies he runs it at
riot, careless of time, place, or any probability. Athenian
lovers are the sport of Warwickshire fairies, who also
play Jack-o'-Lantern with Warwickshire journeymen,
who are devising an entertainment for Athenian royalty.
In *Much Ado,* Dogberry and his Watch slouch in across
the hunt (to quote Raleigh) as unconcernedly as though

Messina were their own Warwickshire. Falstaff is always the foil of Royalty. He has his being on the skirt of royal affairs, whether taverning, taking the field, living to fight another day, raising his ragged regiment or getting his heart broken and dying of it. So the fools, the rusticals, the eccentrics, make sport or commentary—as Autolycus and the Bohemian shepherds: but all, as the saying is, "know their place," and their place is at the tail of the procession.

VI

A typical Comedy of Shakespeare's is, in its *intention,* polite, high-bred, courtly. And because of this there has grown up among moderns who bend their high brows over his *dramatis personae* and count the disproportionate number, as it seems to them, of kings, princes, princesses, dukes and councillors, a curious itch to enquire "Was Shakespeare a Snob?"—an itch which, ignoring history, and the circumstances of the Theatre in Shakespeare's time, betrays a flat imperception of the artistic mind, how it always works; and moreover bears on the reverse of their token-pennies an exact image, turned the other way about, of that snobbery which assumes that the Plays, being what they are, cannot be attributed to a plain commoner, but must attribute them to an Earl of Oxford or of Dorset, or to a Viscount of St. Albans at least—as, in a later age, the Father of Chemistry was brother to the Earl of Cork. For there is, in our day, a Snobbery that adulates the mob and cringes to it, as another worships and cringes to titles. And if we get that into our heads, we can dismiss with a smile the nine-tenths of personal speculation written about Shakespeare today. Shakespeare disliked

a crowd. Don't you? Nay—to put it more particularly
—Shakespeare, as we know, had a most delicate nostril,
to which the fragrance of the violet, of wild thyme,
honeysuckle, lavender, sweet musk roses, appealed as
Heaven-on-earth. He disliked civet among the powders
of the merchants : but the smell of a crowd, with its
stale sweat and garlic (no Cytherea's breath!), was
poison to him and, even in imagination, induced something like a physical nausea.

Again, he was a working playwright, and even for
his pomp and pageantry we could, if excuse were needed,
put up the plainest commercial work-a-day one. His
audiences or his manager liked fine clothes and he had
to write to his Company's Wardrobe, which in those
days was highly expensive and therefore limited, as we
know by preserved inventory.

But set that aside and say, What serious vice lurks in
a taste for ceremonial and high manners, or even in
wanting a coat-of-arms of one's own? Let that be a
gewgaw if you will. But after all, as Coventry Patmore
says, "there is nothing comparable for moral force to
the charm of truly noble manners," and such noble
manners are (or were) at once an appanage and an
obligation of high estate in this realm. Call the aspira-
tion, if you will, an "infirmity of noble minds." Still
it is not ignoble. I challenge you further—it is rightly
universal: we naturally share it, and only by sharing it
can we understand Shakespeare. As Emerson has said,
"All that Shakespeare says of the King, yonder slip of
a boy that reads in the corner feels to be true of himself." Each of us, if worth anything, is thus in mind
potentially royal.

I might say more of critics who, nescient of the
operations of a creative mind, read an artist's work into

his actual life, which is, by degrees of his sublimity, a fainter and fainter shadow of his soul; who condemn Shakespeare's love of courtliness through their own fashionable worship of democracy and congregated nightcaps. But I have digressed enough, and recall myself to the plain fact that a typical Comedy of Shakespeare's is courtly-polite.

VII

Still following our line of exclusion, we may agree that while usually and preferably Italianate in Scenery and setting, with its plot quite as often as not borrowed from an Italian novel or mal-twisted (as in *All's Well*) out of Boccaccio, Shakespeare derives nothing of worth from any Italian Comedy known to us. In *The Taming of the Shrew,* to be sure, he borrows the worst of his plot, by remove, from Ariosto. Now Ariosto was a great poet; and his great Epic, like our Spenser's, a very great Epic indeed, composed in very similar fashion. But the time of any comparable excellence in Drama was not yet, and the Comedies of Ariosto, written to amuse the Court of Ferrara, are—to put it bluntly— very poor stuff and rightly have been put by Benedetto Croce outside of any serious estimate. From Boccaccio —as Chaucer did—or from any later collection of Italian stories, Shakespeare might (and demonstrably did) borrow at will; in *All's Well,* for example, not improving. To the contemporary Italian theatre he owes nothing of worth that the ordinary student can discover.

In speaking of contemporary or somewhat later Spanish and Portuguese Comedy, I must imitate the modesty of Sir John Mandeville when his reported travels should have brought him to the Garden of Eden.

"Of Paradys," he confesses, "ne can I speken properly, for I was not there." So of the theatre of Cervantes and Lope de Vega and of Calderon I cannot speak properly, knowing their plays only through translations and translated fragments. They are polite of course: but, so far as I discover (save for a hint here and there in Calderon), unseasoned by that broad humour which is Shakespeare's specific for "humanising" a polite play. Also they pretty plainly suffer from the pedantic "rules" of Castelvetro who published his (the first) commentary on *The Poetics* of Aristotle in 1570 and interpreting out of his own head an Aristotelian Theory of Comedy which—admitting a wild conjecture that Aristotle once wrote one, we know to have perished and been non-existent in Castelvetro's day as it remains non-existent in ours—actually governed the practice of Comedy on the Continent for generations; governed, in fact, the great French drama of the seventeenth century—Molière himself and his successors. Now this dominating theory of Castelvetro's—*Pedantuccio e grammatuccio* as an angry rival called him—presumed not only to tell you and me how to judge a play, but how to *write* one. According to Castelvetro (who never wrote one) a Comedy must deal ludicrously with harmless moral turpitude: and *therefore* it does not properly touch kings or princes. . . . It may be polite: but the actions of kings belong to tragedy. In his definition, which I use because Molière obeyed it, Comedy should be "the private action of a private citizen. . . . Small injuries, trivial intrigues, especially in love-affairs, make the plots of Comedy. Its *dramatis personae* are of poor spirit, mean estate, and their whole concern is with amorous delights." Now cast your mind back to Shakespeare and say how he smashes down any such definition. Kings and Clowns

jostle on his stage naturally and universally. It takes all
sorts to make Shakespeare's world.[1] Moreover, and before we leave dealing with his preference for courtly
characters, let me remind the "snobbery" theorists of
As You Like It—how delicately, how surely he satirises,
in his own Arden, the exiled Court practising the return-
to-Nature business: how artfully he brings in its two
critics—Jaques in his black, Touchstone in his motley—
who mock one another, but behind their stalking-horses
let fly at their common game from opposite angles. The
Duke is a noble sententious gentleman who makes the
best of it and, when the winter's wind bites and blows
upon his body, can announce:

> This is no flattery: these are counsellors
> That feelingly persuade me what I am.

And his loyal counsellors play up to it on the old habit
of flattery, carolling,

> Blow, blow, thou winter wind!

But *Ducdamè, ducdamè, ducdamè* chants Jaques, and
his oppositor, being questioned, "How like you this
shepherd's life, Master Touchstone," responds:

> Truly, shepherd, in respect of itself it is a good life, but in
> respect that it is a shepherd's life, it is naught . . . etc.

"And this our life"—prosily poetises on the old Duke—

> And this our life, exempt from public haunt,
> Finds tongues in trees. . . .

[1] As later, by the way, it takes all sorts to make Walter Scott's
world.

But it doesn't. It finds ballads *on* trees, and precious
bad ballads at that. And in the end observe that all
these philosophic exiles go contentedly back to the life
which is theirs : as Prospero himself goes back to it.

> The cloud-capped towers, the gorgeous palaces

may be, as he impressively tells us, dissoluble as this
his insubstantial pageant : still—and not I think solely
for his daughter's sake—he sails home to recover and
enjoy them : and Ariel is released to fly down on the
bat's back after Summer—the Island in its fringe of
surf abandoned to Caliban and his scammels—whatever
scammels may be.

VIII

I mentioned Molière just now : and he (I think) may
bring us, still following our method of exclusion, almost
to the secret of our matter.

Molière—I choose him as admittedly the prince of
his tribe—was a consummate playwright and handler of
the comic theme. *But he was no poet.* And if you agree
with me upon almost a last exclusion, we find ourselves
at length on the edge of some definition. Yet still I
warn you. George Meredith, in his well-known Essay
on Comedy, majestically and magisterially assumes the
Molière idea of Comedy (derived through Menander,
of whose work we know nothing save through presumably slavish imitations by Plautus and Terence) to
be the norm of all Comedy, preserved through Regnault,
Congreve, Sheridan, whom you will. But why? What
is the matter with the Old Greek Comedy?—with
Aristophanes who makes the gods talk scandalously

and Socrates meteorologise from a hamper; and Pro-
metheus walk the stage under an umbrella? Molière
may be, if you like, a superior artist to the Aristophanic
Labiche in whose more frolic farces (as Henley puts it,
more or less) the Sphinx is sib to the Cheshire Cat and
all Olympus demoralised by champagne and oysters.
But Labiche is farce, you see, and Aristophanes presumably pantomime, and even the stuff of *The Arabian
Nights* not rightly Comic Material. "There is fun in
Baghdad" (Why not?); but it will not fit into Meredith's
theory, which you may summarise as Menander-Molière.
So out go the Caliph, the hunchback, the barber; out
goes Aristophanes; out goes the Baby with the Bath;
and out goes Shakespeare. Heroic jettison for the sake
of a definition!

IX

Molière within his chosen limits—the limits of what
his countrymen call *Sagesse*—is a consummate comic
writer: Shakespeare sometimes consummate, often not,
having no limits: but greater *because he had no limits,*
because he was a tremendous poet and Molière (I repeat) no poet at all.

Now I am not going to be caught in Meredith's trap
and attempt a definition of Poetry as he of Comedy.
True poetry is what the poets write: beyond that, an
indefinable thing and untranslatable (say) as the opening
Chorus of Aristophanes' *Clouds*. Like a cloud it comes
up over our horizon, overtakes, overcomes us: not to
be outlined, but recognisable. Suppose Shakespeare to
be talking of Fairies. We open an earlier play of his and
read this:

And never, since the middle summer's Spring,
Met we on hill, in dale, forest, or mead,
By pavèd fountain, or by rushy brook,
Or in the beachéd margent of the sea,
To dance our ringlets to the whistling wind. . . .

or we open on his last and read:

Ye elves of hills, brooks, standing lakes and groves,
And ye that on the sands with printless foot
Do chase the ebbing Neptune, and do fly him
When he comes back. . . .

Casually again we open a page of *All's Well* and hear the sick king speaking to Helena of her dead father, the wise physician:

Would I were with him! He would always say—
Methinks I hear him now: his plausive words
He scattered not in ears, but grafted them
To grow there and to bear: "Let me not live—"
Thus his good melancholy oft began,
On the castastrophe and heel of pastime
When it was out—"Let me not live," quoth he,
"After my flame lacks oil, to be the snuff
Of younger spirits, whose apprehensive senses
All but new things disdain: whose judgments are
Mere fathers of their garments—

(I humbly with Tyrwhitt conjecture 'feathers')

Mere feathers of their garments; whose constancies
Expire before their fashions." This he wished:
I, after him, do after him wish too;
Since I nor wax nor honey can bring home
I quickly were dissolvèd from my hive
To give some labourers room. . . .

I fill a place, I know it. . . .

Well, now, such passages as those are unchallenge-
able poetry. Upon the last quoted I would ask you to
consider if Shakespeare did not instinctively choose
great princes and princesses for his drama—Tragedy or
Comedy—because they *ought* to talk in that magnificent
way. I say not that they do: we know very well that
George the Third, for one, did not. But, as Aristotle
has justly observed, Poetry concerns itself with things
not as they happen but as in the right nature of things
they should happen.

And of all these passages I ask you to observe that
their poetry differs totally from the slight, pretty accomplishment of Lyly (say) or of Beaumont and
Fletcher. It has a deeper resonance: it carries a deeper
import in its over-tones and under-tones—at times an
unearthly import. The elves on the sands

> with printless foot
> Do chase the ebbing Neptune, and do fly him—

"with printless foot," but (to quote poor John Davidson) :

> Weave the dance and sing the song!
> Subterranean depths prolong
> The rainy patter of our feet. . . .

"Where should this music be? I' th' air or th' earth?"
demands bewildered Ferdinand, Ariel taboring above
him; to be answered by its echo *Ding, dong!* tolled deep
down in the caves of the sea.

Music? The Comedies as you know are haunted by
actual music, not only by music of the spoken voice,

which at any point may melt into music. Music may
come in pertinently, as when played beneath Silvia's
balcony, or in Belmont's moonlit garden; less pertinently,
as when in *Much Ado* a singing-boy is introduced to
delight us with "Sigh no more, ladies"; or quite impertinently, as when, in *As You Like It*, two lads happen
along and give us "It was a lover and his lass." Yet why
do I say "impertinently," when it just fits in? It is
music, but it is also sunlight playing over the acres of
the young corn. Have you ever noted—no, I beg your
pardon, for of course you have—how Shakespeare can
make music carry a desired effect of light, so that the
two are by our senses indivisible?—as when the Boy
sings to Mariana in the moated garden:

> Take, oh take those lips away,

and we see, as it were through a rift of copperous
thunder clouds, the dusk gathering over a landscape far
and forlorn.

But the play in which the music and sweet poetry best
agree is admittedly that Comedy of Comedies *Twelfth
Night*. It opens, it closes to music, and music winds by
its fountains, arbours, all its pleasant alleys. I call it the
Comedy of Comedies not merely as indicating my own
preference (challengeable only by *The Tempest*) but as a
casket enclosing so many memories of Shakespeare at
his liveliest—spring, youth, love, lustihead, practical jok-
ing. I think of Herbert's

> Sweet Spring, full of sweet days and roses,
> A box where sweets compacted lie,
> My music shows ye have your closes
>   And all must die.

Music and light again: but in this play it is music and moonlight: and in its lunar garden so many ghosts reincarnate themselves!—Falstaff in Sir Toby, Silly Slender in Sir Andrew, all the Court of Navarre in the love-sick Duke, in Viola all the heroines that put on man's clothing; in Feste with his songs, all the wisdom of many Fools: and he, like his cousin, Lear's poor Fool, is left shivering:

> When that I was and a little tiny boy,
>   With hey, ho, the wind and the rain;
> A foolish thing was but a toy,
>   For the rain it raineth every day. . . .
> A great while ago the world begun,
>   With hey, ho, the wind and the rain:
> But that's all one, our play is done. . . .

Finis rerum! and

> We'll go no more a-roving
> By the light of the moon.

Two words more on this matter of Music before I pass from it.

(1) It has sometimes occurred to me that Shakespeare used it often to help out the poverty of his scenic Theatre. But on the other hand I am sure that we are misled if, trusting to that silly old picture of an Elizabethan stage reproduced in every text-book, we imagine that scenery did not immensely develop during Shakespeare's time—that a balcony with an alcove under it, two doors and a placard "A Wood near Athens" or "Another part of the Field" sufficed for staging *Pericles* or *The Tempest*. Ask yourselves, "Is it likely that in

that teeming time, with dramatists, managers competing hectically for public favour, the art of the scene-painter and of the stage-carpenter stood still?" Or, if you can swallow this human improbability, ask yourself, "Is it credible that this primitive apparatus burst all of a sudden into the elaborate machinery devised by Inigo Jones for Ben Jonson's Masques?" I submit that it is not credible.

(2) Secondly, it is the last test of greatness that, persisting, it awes successive generations in various ways and through different virtues. Shakespeare has mastered men in turn by his winningness, his majesty, his grip of character, his knowledge of the human heart. I think he masters this, our, generation most by the magic and music of a way of speaking which makes all things new.

X

The gap of time between *Twelfth Night* and *The Tempest* (as all the years from the five greatest Tragedies to the end) is occupied by plays which give men excuse for talk of Shakespeare's "declining powers" and speculations upon that decline in a scarce-elderly man. Now setting aside the fallacy that a great artist should, must, or can go continuously from strength to strength in a kind of mathematical progression, yet observing that natural instinct which impels great artists (and all great conquerors for that matter) to attempt new conquests *because* they are difficult, we may discount this theory of "declining powers" and even dismiss it, *when once we discover what Shakespeare was attempting.*

He was attempting (as elsewhere I have tried at length to prove) the apparently impossible; putting his fate and fame to the touch upon it too. For some

reason his mind during these years brooded on the problem—the dramatic problem—of Reconciliation: how to
appease the sins, quarrels, follies of the fathers in the
loves of their children, and do it in "the two or three
hours' traffic of our stage"—to do in short precisely that
which Sir Philip Sidney, in a famous passage, had de-
rided. Early in his career, in *Romeo and Juliet,* he was
haunted by this dramatic problem of Reconciliation, and
in the prologue of that play protested its difficulty:

> Two households, both alike in dignity,
>   In fair Verona, where we lay our scene,
> From ancient grudge break to new mutiny,
>   Where civil blood makes civil hands unclean.
> From forth the fatal loins of these two foes
>   A pair of star-cross'd lovers take their life;
> Whose misadventur'd piteous overthrows
>   Do with their death bury their parents' strife.
> The fearful passage of their death-mark'd love,
>   And the continuance of their parents' rage,
> Which, but their children's end, nought could remove,
>   Is now the two hours' traffic of our stage;
> The which if you with patient ears attend,
> What here shall miss, our toil shall strive to mend.

Reconciliation is naturally a slow process: to make a
small boy and a small girl come to birth, grow up, fall
in love and reconcile their parents in the space of two
or three hours is (one would say) an impossible process.
But

> To find out what you cannot do
> And then to go and do it:
> There lies the golden rule . . .

—in art. Once, twice, thrice he tried—in *Pericles,* in *Cymbeline,* in *The Winter's Tale,* using various devices to annihilate time: and then in *The Tempest,* partly through magic, he brought it off: after which feat Prospero might break his wand and sink his book.

XI

I shall conclude with one or two quite homely and practical words on reading Shakespeare; of advice not derived from any scholarship to which I shrink from pretending, but from a life-long enjoyment. And I say, since Shakespeare wrote to be acted, visit what performances of him you can. Our present ones may be wrong; but our present performers are doing their best, and their efforts continue his perpetuity. But as the true classical scholar takes a small Pindar or Horace in pocket or haversack, so carry a thin volume of Shakespeare in yours. His text is, in many plays, manifestly corrupt. (Heaven may even have contrived it so for us, to be all the better fun.) Keep your honesty, of course: and when you come on a passage unconstruable or beyond emendation after many attempts, just say—as Samuel Johnson never scrupled to say (and it makes him the wisest of all commentators)—"I can make nothing of this Passage." Do not send your conjectures to *The Times* "Literary Supplement." Just keep them to yourself and revise them.

Shall I say hardily that provided we eschew, so far as possible, conjectural *emendation*—remembering Aldis Wright's assertion that "in most cases ignorance and conceit are its fruitful parents"—but allowing ourselves some range of conjectural *interpretation*—we can so combine entertainment with an innocent certainty that

little harm is done even when we are wrong. A friend
of mine, an old Squire of Devon, used to demonstrate
to me at great length that when Shakespeare wrote of
the moon looking,

> "With a watery eye"—
> And when she weeps, weeps every little flower,
> Lamenting some enforced chastity—

he anticipated our modern knowledge of plant-fertili-
sation. Good man, he took "enforced" to mean "compulsory"; and I never dared to dash his enthusiasm
by hinting that, as Shakespeare would use the word
"enforced," an "enforced chastity" meant a chastity
violated.

I suggested, just now, a conjectural emendation in
All's Well—"feathers" for "fathers"—which, since I
find that Tyrwhitt is the only one before me, is probably
quite wrong. For a prettier instance perhaps—I was
boggling, one day, over that famous crux in *The
Tempest* where Prospero says:

> Now does my project gather to a head:
> My charms crack not: my spirits obey, *and
> Time
> Goes upright with his carriage.* (*To Ariel*)
> How's the day?
>
> *Ariel.* On the sixth hour, at which time, my lord,
> You said our work should cease.

Now if we go back to Act 1, Scene 2, we find Prospero
and Ariel similarly conning the hour as if meaning us
to note the time circumscribing the magic.

> There's more work,
> What is the time o' th' day?

demands the wizard hurriedly.   Ariel glances at the sun's altitude.

> Past the mid season

—afternoon, that is.   Prospero pulls out his watch:

> At least two glasses—The time 'twixt *six* and now
> Must by us both be spent most preciously.

They "make it so," as the sailors say.   Then at six they "make it so" again.   This time Prospero is nervous and first consults his watch.

> Time
> Goes upright with his carriage . . . How's the day?
> On the sixth hour.

If you will consult your watches, you will find that six o'clock is the one moment in the twelve when the hour and minute hands stand precisely perpendicular and Time is upright in the watch that carries it.   When I put this to a learned friend, he would have none of it, and perhaps he was right.

But I put it to you that without setting ourselves up to be learned commentators, if we soak ourselves in Shakespeare and do not give ourselves airs, these little guesses and apprehensions may be a reserved reward and fun of the thing.   After all, he wrote for enjoyment: we shall never be wise about him unless we take him in that category; and the end of our wisdom is to learn his ways and affectionately puzzle out, behind a perhaps happily dim text, of which he was careless, the meaning of his subtle, sometimes troubled but for us always friendly, smile.

You observe that I have just asked you to consult your watches: a stage-direction for me to make an end before luncheon time.

COVENTRY PATMORE

COVENTRY KERSEY DIGHTON PATMORE was born July 23, 1823. His great-grandmother— a Miss Maria Böckmann, or Baeckmann, sister of a fairly well-known German artist—married a Mr. John Stevens, bringing to the blood of a sound middle-class British family just that foreign strain which is often found to thicken, instead of diluting, its indigenous qualities and breed John Bulls of the burliest convictions and prejudices. Her daughter, Maria Clarissa Stevens, was born in 1761, married in 1783 Mr. Peter Patmore, a jeweller on Ludgate Hill, and died in her ninety-third year of a tumble down-stairs.

Peter and Maria Clarissa Patmore had one child, Peter George, and probably "spoiled" him. At an early age he refused to enter the family business, embarked on a literary career, and became a writer of some note, though he is only remembered now through his unhappy connection with the notorious duel between Mr. John Scott, editor of the *London Magazine,* and Mr. Christie, the friend of Lockhart. He married in 1822 a Miss Eliza Robertson. Coventry Patmore was the first-born of their four children.

The mother is presented to us as a dour and strait-laced woman, a Presbyterian with Puritanical views of life: the father as a vain, showy man, ill-balanced rather than ill-intentioned—as appears clearly enough in the account of the duel and its consequences. Up to this point he had been something of a dandy in dress and opinions: he sobers down to a man who has erred, has righted himself—though not in the world's opinion— and is left nursing a grievance. Thirty-two years after the duel he is still preparing memoranda with a view to a public vindication of his conduct. Such men cannot bear the exceedingly bitter truth that the world, having summed them up justly or unjustly, has lost interest, but without forgetting its verdict. His friends seem to have been faithful to him, but (unless I misread his story) he and they must have felt that his literary career had "gone under." Perhaps—it has happened to many a disappointed but not ignoble man—his hopes passed from himself to fasten the more eagerly on his clever eldest son. At any rate, he keeps our esteem as a devoted father and tender husband. He respected his wife's religious convictions, but had none of his own; disavowed all belief in the supernatural, and would not allow her to impart her views to the children. Young Coventry therefore from the first "could look for no sympathy from his father in those spiritual intuitions, religious aspirations, and vague yearnings after the ideal by which his early youth was haunted." This apart, the two became close companions: the father proud of the boy, eager to indulge his wishes, fostering especially his literary tastes, and in the smallest details of conduct advising him anxiously, yet with frankness, as one secure of being understood.

The Patmores were in easy circumstances, and it was of his father's choice that Coventry spent his boyhood at home. At sixteen he entered a school—a branch of the Collège de France—at St. Germains, in order to improve his French; but did not like it, and returned after a year with an antipathy which lasted his lifetime and kept him consistently unjust towards anything a Frenchman might say or do. His father not only directed his reading, but encouraged a love of the theatre, and took him to visit his literary acquaintances. He was welcomed by such *coteries* as the Basil Montagus' and the Procters', and formed friendships—with Monckton Milnes and Tennyson—afterwards valuable to him in many ways. Also he made the acquaintance of Leigh Hunt—in circumstances which he must be allowed to tell:

I (being, at seventeen or eighteen years of age, or perhaps younger, an admirer of the *Indicator* and *Rimini*) set off with a letter from my father, an old friend of the poet, informing him of my ambition to see him. Arriving at his house, a very small one, in a small square somewhere in the extreme west, after a walk of some five or six miles, I was informed that the poet was at home, and asked to sit down until he came to me. This he did after I had waited in the little parlour at least two hours, when the door was opened and a most picturesque gentleman, with hair flowing nearly or quite to his shoulders, a beautiful velvet coat, and a Vandyke collar of lace about a foot deep, appeared, rubbing his hands and smiling ethereally, and saying, without a word of preface or notice of my having waited so long, "This is a beautiful world, Mr. Patmore!" I was so struck by this remark that it has eclipsed all memory of what occurred during the remainder of my visit.

The boy, in short, was meant by his proud father to be a "somebody," though along what line he was to attain distinction did not appear. He began to write verses: then a craze for science ousted the Muse, and his father fitted up a laboratory for him in a disused kitchen in their London house. For a time he blended his mathematical and scientific work with the study of philosophy, especially of Plato, and of theology, which had for some time been attracting him in spite of his parent. The scientific fit passed. He fell back on a close study of poetry. He conceived and laid aside a notion of taking Orders in the English Church. His father proposed Cambridge. Then in 1842, "the publication of Tennyson's collected poems reawakened the poetic ambition which had for some time laid dormant," and the lad was taken to read before P. G. Patmore's literary allies such poems as he had written. The audience encouraged him, and his father urged him to write enough to fill a volume. This he did in some haste, and the little book was launched in 1844.

Of its contents I am only acquainted with those poems which Patmore allowed to reappear in later collections; but these on the whole awaken no regret for the lost ones. Their author used afterwards to speak of them as trash and an object lesson in faults of style and subject. Yet on the whole the critics received them with respect, and there are lines and even whole stanzas in *The River* and the *Woodman's Daughter* (both written at sixteen) which unmistakably declare the poet. The scenery in the former is aptly and easily painted, and gives us an early assurance of a gift which Patmore afterwards hid somewhat obstinately, yet refined in secret, until, when we come to the *Odes,* we hardly know whether to admire more his penetrating vision for "natural" beauty or his classical economy in the use of it. Nor could a youth without the root of poetry in him have found so exquisite a phrase for girlhood as

The sweet age
When heaven's our side the lark.

But weak in choice of subject, and loose in their grip of it, these poems undoubtedly are. And (to anticipate a little) I find the same feebleness, poorly disguised by wayward abruptness and obscurity, in *Tamerton Church Tower*. It would be false for me to pretend that, after several readings, I understand that poem, or even know precisely what it is all about. Now Patmore, in an essay on "Obscure Books," warns us against shirking or condemning an author merely because he is obscure: but in his essay on Blake he tells us with equal wisdom that "a sensible person can easily distinguish between that which he cannot understand and that in which there is nothing to be understood." I am far from saying that in the ill-told and apparently aimless story of *Tamerton Church Tower* there is nothing to be understood; but I certainly do not find the intelligible portion of it either so pleasant or so profitable as to awaken the smallest desire to explore the rest. It is, let me grant, a "noticeable" poem; but it is also a very callous one, and (worse than this) it treats of women with a short-sighted vulgarity most singular to find in a young poet destined to become the singer of wedlock and married love.

But between the dates of these early poems and *Tamerton Church Tower* a great deal had happened. P. G. Patmore had been managing his own and his wife's property with less care or ability than he gave to advancing his son. To recover his position he began to speculate rashly in railway stock—in the fatal year '45. Soon the crash came, and he ran to his friend, the younger Hazlitt, for advice. "Hazlitt," he demanded "what in God's name am I to do? I am in for a million." "Do?" returned Hazlitt. "Why, stay where you are; they know well enough you haven't got it." Patmore, however, quitted England, and the sons were left to fend for themselves.

Coventry appears to have done so most gamely. It was a severe test for a young man who had never known the want of money or missed the indulgence of a whim. But he and his younger brother Gurney contrived to subsist on writing for the magazines and translating. "He managed to scrape together some twenty-five shillings a week, often working for it, as he said, not less than sixteen hours a day." The strain lasted for fifteen months and his health was suffering, when Mr. Monckton Milnes (afterwards Lord Houghton) came to the rescue and obtained for him the post of an assistant in the Library of the British Museum. (As a distinguished novelist quaintly put it to me soon after Lord Houghton's death, "If all the men whom Milnes helped were to choose the same moment and say, 'He was good to me,' this small world would send up a big shout.") In the British Museum Coventry Patmore worked from 1846 till the beginning of 1866, a shy man, holding himself aloof, diligent, though not specially qualified. In 1851 he came out of his shell for a time, and persuaded his colleagues at the Museum to start a rifle club. England at the time (the reader will remember the opening chapter of Mr. Meredith's *Beauchamp's Career*) was suspicious of Louis Napoleon, and had been irritated, if not seriously alarmed, by the vapourings of certain French colonels—"wide red breeches blown out by Fame"—in response to our criticism of their new sovereign. Ignoring the inalienable right of this island-race to advise its neighbours for their good, they so far forgot themselves as to advise us to mend our manners, in default of which, one general even promised to march on London with ten thousand men and teach us.

Patmore, true citizen, followed up his practical essay in patriotism with a letter addressed to *The Times*. Tennyson took up the cry, and wrote and published in the same paper his *Riflemen, form!* The Government at first, and as a matter of course, discouraged the rifle club experiments, but shortly afterwards issued a national appeal. The result was the Volunteer Movement, and of his share in it Patmore never ceased to be proud.

His first book of poems had attracted the notice and won the admiration of Rossetti and other Pre-Raphaelites—then a struggling brotherhood. In 1849 he made their acquaintance, sympathised in great measure with their aims, and helped them, not only by poetising in the *Germ,* but by enlisting his friend Ruskin to take up the cudgels and send to *The Times* his famous letters championing Millais and Holman Hunt. In this he did true service, and it rewarded him with some life-long friendships; but he never belonged to the Brotherhood. He nursed his own aims; and after a time, without any definite breach, he drifted away from his old associates.

He nursed his own aims; and now many circumstances united to give them shape, and bend his mind upon what he came to believe, and thereafter persistently believed, to be his true mission in the world. He had become a convinced Christian; and, like Milton, he "devoted" himself to improving the talent by which he felt he could best serve his Maker and his fellow-men. He desired to write *"the* poem of the day," and to that end set himself down to master, by severe study, all the intricacies of the poetic art. Such devotion does not imply that the devotee has chosen his subject. Milton had prepared himself arduously for many years before discovering his great theme. Patmore's early experiments had revealed— and he was conscious of it, perhaps—a peculiar fallibility in subject. But on May 17, 1847, and at the fortunate moment, he became engaged to Emily Augusta Andrews, and married her on September 11. In the exaltation of the married lover his theme was revealed to him. He was to be the Poet of Nuptial Love. He attempted nothing in haste. Long afterwards he could say of his work, and with perfect truth, "I have written little, but it is all my best: I have never spoken when I had nothing to say, nor spared time or labour to make my words true." But his purpose never faltered. *Tamerton Church Tower* appeared in 1853; three parts of *The Angel in the House* (*The Betrothal, The Espousal,* and *Faithful for Ever*) in 1854, 1856, 1860. In 1863, *The Victories of Love* brought to a close this, the most continuous poetic impulse of his life. The wise and amiable woman who had inspired and sustained it was dead, a year before.

I hinted just now that *Tamerton Church Tower*— which Mr. Champneys, his friend and biographer[1], calls "a sort of preliminary canter"—was a most inauspicious performance. On second thoughts "inauspicious" is not the word. The wine was there, though turbid and even muddy. In the *Angel* it has been clarified by time and quiet thinking; the lees have settled; the liquor is drained off bright and pure. The one poem tells us little and tells it darkly; the other attempts far more, yet remains exquisitely perspicuous. The one has the capriciousness of imperfect insight; the other delivers a story rounded and complete. Its completeness is but the converse of Patmore's thoroughness in thinking out his subject; its perspicuity comes not only of clear apprehension but of sincere feeling. The *Angel* achieved popularity, and

[1] *Memoirs and Correspondence of Coventry Patmore.* By Basil Champneys. 2 vols. London: George Bell and Sons. 1900.

endeared itself to thousands who cared little for poetry
as poetry; and any one who chooses can deride this
popularity and discover unintelligent reasons for it. The
poem dealt with emotions through which most of us pass
at one time or another, and in passing through which (as
almost any breach of promise case will prove) the most
prosaic of God's creatures finds a temporary solace in the
Muse.   Patmore looked into these emotions with clear
eyes, but he spoke of them with a decency which was
even more gratifying to a race accustomed to value
decency above insight.   British poetry contains a very
great deal of information about love, some of it really
illuminating: but the language is frequently ill-regu-
lated, and its authors have too often allowed their
passions to run on unworthy objects, not to say hussies.
What a relief, then, to come across an author who sings
of love as "connected with the clergy"! What a comfort for the respectably betrothed to find their passions
guaranteed by the daughter of an Anglican dean!

I have listened to such derisive attempts to account for
the poem's popularity, and believe that they miss the
truth.   I believe that what actually won a way for it was
its entire sincerity.   The story is simple and pleasant, yet
to persons unaccustomed to poetry I do not think the
book can be easy reading.   It contains (especially in the
Preludes) a large amount of abstract thought. Patmore's
Muse, when she *did* alight or tread the earth, was as yet
(for I am speaking of the *Angel,* not of the *Odes*) apt
to go flat-footedly; and an untrained reader dislikes and
shirks abstract thought.   By its strength the author's
emotion lifts the reader over these difficulties; by its
clearness of conviction it provides him with eyes.   It
achieves, and surely in its climax transmits, the true
lover's thrill.   And it leaves you with an after-taste of

hours spent in company both amiable and profitable, an impression which I may liken to a memory of some sunny morning-room, fresh, habitable, and decorously gay with English flowers.

Patmore had convinced himself, and remained convinced, that nuptial love contains the key, for men and women, of spiritual truth; that, things which are unseen being apprehended from things which are seen, the love between man and woman is the true stair by which alone we can mount to an apprehension of the love of God. Extending this belief into art and literature, he held that in nuptial love the painter and the poet must find the highest of all themes. I state this view of his not so much to contest it, as to point out some conditions imposed on it by the material and methods of art. We regard nuptial love at its best as peaceful, as normal, as a state in which two different natures with two separate wills acquiesce in equipoise. Now, no one has spoken more weightily than Patmore of the value of peace in art, of that restfulness which abides in the normal, in order, in law, and (subjectively) in obedience to law. But arts such as painting and poetry illustrate law by means of its exceptions, vindicate the normal by means of man's deflections from it, teach peace by bringing it triumphant out of conflict. They work, in short, by comparison and contrast. "Shakespeare," says Patmore, "evolves peace from the conflict of interests and passions to which the predominance and victory of a moral idea give unity. That idea is never embodied in any single conspicuous character, though it is usually allowed an unobtrusive expression in some subordinate personality, in order to afford a clue to the 'theme' of the whole harmony. Such theme-suggesting characters are, for example, the Friar in *Romeo and Juliet,* and Kent in

King Lear, who represent and embody the law *from which all the other characters depart more or less, with proportionate disaster to themselves ."* In other words, the normal is art's standard and point of reference rather than its subject-matter. We test the other characters by Kent, but he is never our protagonist: we establish our theme by lessons drawn from those who are unlike Kent.

If this be true, then nuptial love, treated absolutely, is as poor a subject for art as, treated relatively, it is a good one; and poets and dramatists have been wise in building on its perturbations, keeping its normal calm in the background as a law by which to test the unhappiness or disaster of rebels. And therefore I cannot help thinking that, pleasant as we find it when Felix and Honoria arrive in port after their gentle agitations, Patmore would have found it extremely difficult to build a poem on their subsequent bliss, and that with the *Victories of Love*—in which their happiness forms a point of rest— he discovered in the less complacent yoke of Frederick and Jane a far better subject, if he had only handled it well.

It is cast in the form of letters, supposed to pass between the principal characters and their confidants; and these letters run up and down the gamut of artifice, from the meanest trivialities of realism to "diction" in its remotest degrees; from

>   My dearest niece, I'm charm'd to hear
>   The scenery's fine at Windermere. . . .

to

>   Nature's infinite ostent
>   Of lovely flowers in wood and mead
>   That weet not whether any heed.

Reviewers did not omit to make merry over such lines as "My dearest niece, I'm charm'd to hear"; and undoubtedly too much prominence has been given to Patmore's feats in the Art of Sinking; but that he could be profoundly bathetic and serenely unconscious of bathos he demonstrated once and sufficiently for all time with his poem *The Rosy Bosom'd Hours*—

> A florin to the willing guard
>   Secured, for half the way,
> (He lock'd us in, ah, lucky-starr'd)
>   A curtain'd front coupé.

not only by writing it, but by allowing it to be included as a representative poem, in a little volume edited for popular use by Professor Henry Morley, and published by Messrs. Cassell and Co. in 1888. One word more about the *Angel* and *Victories of Love*. I have always found it difficult to reconcile the deep and tender homage paid to woman in these poems, and notably in the lines beginning

> Why, having won her, do I woo?

and ending—

> Because her gay and lofty brows,
>   When all is won that hope can ask,
> Reflect a light of hopeless snows
>   That bright in virgin ether bask;
> Because, though free of the outer court
>   I am, this temple keeps its shrine
> Sacred to Heaven; because, in short,
>   She's not and never can be mine,

with the opinions on the natural subjection of woman persistently held by Patmore, and expounded in his prose essays. In them he never tires of scoffing at the view of woman as man's equal, though dissimilar. She is the "weaker vessel," "the last and lowest of all spiritual creatures," made to be ruled and strictly ruled: "No right-minded woman would care a straw for her lover's adoration if she did not know that he knew that after all he was the true divinity"—with much more to the same effect. How, then, does man arrive at paying homage and reverence to that which is of so much less worth and dignity than he? Apparently by a magnificent act of condescension. "The myth of King Cophetua and the Beggar-maid is representative of the most perfect nuptial relationship." So in the poem *King Cophetua the First* Jove finds tiresomeness in "Juno's almost equal mind," and descends

> On low and little Earth to seek
> That vessel infinitely weak
> (The abler for the infinite honour
> He hugely long'd to put upon her).

This condescension is, no doubt, mighty fine; but when the lordly wooer begins to talk of "hopeless snows" and "unscaleable altitudes" in the creature to whom he stoops, he is (*ex hypothesi*) uttering an untruth. The woman (I gather) knows it to be untrue and "an infatuation of love on the part of the giver." And this again is mighty pretty, and we gather (with just a tinge of regret) that when Felix sung so handsomely of Honoria's "hopeless snows," it was "only his fun," and Honoria knew it, and "there are few more damnable heresies than the doctrine of the equality of man and woman." Very well; but carry up this analogy, as Patmore did, and boldly apply it to divine love, and you are face to face with the idea of an infatuated God, a God who (consciously or unconsciously) abandons supreme strength and sanity for weakness and delusion in His passion for the elect soul and His pursuit of her. I believe I am uttering nothing here to which Patmore would not have subscribed. To him the Almighty was the Divine Lover depicted in the old ballad *Quia Amore Langueo*—

> I am true love that false was never;
> > My sister, man's soul, I loved her thus.
> Because we would in no wise dissever,
> > I left my kingdom glorious.
> I purveyed her a palace full precious;
> > She fled, I followed; I loved her so
> That I suffered this pain piteous,
> > *Quia amore langueo*.

For me (if it be not immodest to obtrude my opinion on a question so much more serious than any which I set out to discuss) this philosophy of Patmore's replaces by a conscious make-believe the honesty I should require at the foot of the ascent, and at the summit robs the Almighty of that infinitely deep celestial peace towards which the wisest of Christians and heathens have lifted their eyes. But (to return to the small business of literary criticism) it is, I confess, a disappointment to discover that the exquisite homage paid to Honoria by her poet-husband was, after all, polite humbug. "Everybody knew what he meant in thus making a divinity of her," etc. Did everybody? I—alas!—for years understood him to be saying what he believed. Nor am I assured that Patmore knew everything about love when I read *Amelia* (which, with his rifle club, he reckoned

his greatest achievement), and note the chill conde-
scension beneath the exquisite phrasing of that idyll—
so perfect in expression, so fundamentally selfish and
patronising in its point of view. Nor, again, am I sure
that in chivalry he had hold of the right end of the stick,
when I read *The Storm,* and learn how he earned the
thanks of his Beloved by running home in the rain, and
sending her "woman" with an umbrella!

Emily Patmore died in the summer of 1862. The
coincidence of the blow with the close of the long poetic
task in which she had been at once his fount of inspiration, his model, and the practical nurse of his energies,
seems to have thrown him off his balance. For the
moment everything had come to an end. A widower,
with a young family; a poet, with a task accomplished
and no future one planned; a religious man caught in an
interval of hesitation between two creeds—he felt that
his hand had suddenly lost grasp of the old continuous
threads, and that he must darkly fumble for new ones.
He found two such in a new religion and a second wife.
In 1864 he visited Rome, not without an *arrière pensée*
that this visit might decide that plunge into the Roman
Catholic Church towards which (and in spite of his wife's
restraining hand) he had long been drifting. At Rome
he made the acquaintance of a Miss Mary Byles, an English convert of Manning's. She became the confidante of
his spiritual troubles, and in a short time he made her a
proposal of marriage.

Miss Byles possessed a considerable fortune, but
Patmore did not know this at the time. The knowledge,
when imparted to him, almost broke off their engage-
ment. But good sense triumphed, and when once
Patmore had brought himself to accept his worldly good
fortune, his patriarchal view of the relations between

husband and wife obliged him to undertake cheerfully, and even enthusiastically, the management of his wife's property. He fully expected that his new marriage and change of religion would cost him many friends. It appears that they actually did; though the severest loss— the breach of his intimacy with Tennyson—can be accounted for by neither, and seems, on the evidence, to be wholly chargeable to Tennyson's discredit. In 1865 Patmore retired from the British Museum. In the following year an estate—Heron's Ghyll—was bought in Sussex; Patmore became the complete man of business, and threw himself heart and soul into the task of converting the farmhouse into a healthy, habitable, and comely country residence, laying out and planting the grounds about it, farming the outlying three-hundred-odd acres, and generally improving the estate and enhancing its value. His wife, it is clear, behaved beautifully. One does not gather that hers was a happy life; but, though intensely reserved and "old maidish," she won the affection of her husband's children by sheer goodness, and faltered in duty neither towards them nor towards him. She could trust him as a judicious steward of the wealth she had brought, and he was happy. Says Mr. Champneys in a chapter of "Personal Recollections":

It was evident that Patmore thoroughly and constantly enjoyed the relief from straitened means. No money was spared on the estate, though none was wasted. He freely indulged his taste for pet animals; kept as good a head of game on his property as it would hold, at a quite disproportionate cost; and among the smaller luxuries which he allowed himself was the lavish use of logs in the wood fires which were kept going in all but the hottest days. I can even now recall his tall figure striding into the drawing-room from his books or letters, taking up his characteristic position, the back against the mantelpiece, the tails of his velvet shoot-coat under his arms, a kind of shake and shiver, like that of one of his favourite Newfoundlands just out of the water; the turn towards the fire, and the liberal piling on of logs, which was in no degree checked by a gentle reminder from his wife how much they cost him, a remonstrance which he met only by a tolerant smile. Then he would, as the fire burnt up, bask to his content, and one felt that the genial sense of easy circumstances was probably more of the essence of his enjoyment than physical warmth.

It would be hard to say precisely how these changed conditions of life affected his development as a poet. At first they seem to have deadened all impulse to write; but it revived, and in 1868 we find him printing the first instalment of the *Odes* for private circulation among his friends. The springs were loosened again, but the stream ran far less copiously than before. He had his own explanation for this: "Not to run before he is sent is the first duty of a poet, and that which all living poets—except Barnes—forget. If this duty is religious-ly kept, a very little running may make the successful race, when the moment for starting comes." And again: "I am the only poet of this generation, except Barnes, who has steadily maintained a literary conscience." As Mr. Champneys more than once reminds us, Patmore was always optimistic about his own affairs; but in justice we must admit—I believe every thoughtful lover of poetry will admit—that the released spring, though a *fons tenuis,* yielded a diviner, if less popular, drink than in the gushing days of *The Angel in the House.*

The *Odes* stole quietly upon the world, at intervals; and the world has been slow in awaking to the sense of its gain. Gradually, however, the opinion gains that we possess in them one of the rarest treasures of Victorian poetry. They are at once so pregnant and so poignant; clouded with thought, yet riven with flashes which penetrate so deeply into heaven, that even his sworn admirers were perplexed by them, hardly knowing what to make of writings so unexpectedly different from the *Angel,* with its easy movement and pervasive everyday atmosphere. Also it must be owned that the *Odes* are of very unequal inspiration. Roughly, they fall into two classes, the one concerned with principles, the other with persons. And here we may bring the *Odes* and the *Prose Writings* under a common criticism. No writer of his generation had a clearer vision than Patmore for truth of principle: I had almost said a vision comparable with his. There are passages in the two little books, *Principle in Art* and *Religio Poetæ,* which every young follower of art should commit to memory and bind for a phylactery on his forehead. But they jostle with passages of the ineptest criticism; for this seer into mysteries was constitutionally incapable of applying the principles he discovered, and of bringing either fair judgment or temperate language to bear upon men and their works. At one moment we are listening to words of most luminous wisdom on the value of rest in art. We turn the page, and read that nowadays "Novels and poems are read, understood, and talked about by young ladies *which Rochester would have blushed to be found reading,* and which Swift would have called indecent"—an overstatement which stifles by violence the small amount of truth it contains, since the persuasiveness of a blushing Rochester is lost in our instant sense of absurdity. So with the *Odes.*— It is well to begin by separating those which take hold of the doors of Heaven from those which exhaust themselves in constructive damnation of Mr. Gladstone.

Somewhere and somehow Patmore had picked up a conception of himself as a stern unbending aristocrat, abandoned by the cowards of his order, but erect, mailed, and defiant among the ruins of that fairer England he and his had ruled so long for its good. The conception is dignified and picturesque, and one which it pleased him immensely to contemplate; but it has no discoverable basis in fact. Mr. Champneys, on being asked his opinion of Mr. Sargent's famous portrait (now hanging in the National Portrait Gallery), replied that if the picture had been extended downwards there must have appeared the handle of a whip. Patmore would then have been revealed as a sort of Southern planter on the point of thrashing his slaves and exclaiming, "You damned niggers!" It is, in fact, just such a portrait as Patmore invites us to draw from certain of the *Odes*.

But in the rest—in *Saint Valentine's Day, Wind and Wave, Winter, The Day after To-morrow, Tristitia, The Azalea, Departure, The Toys, If I Were Dead, Tired Memory,* and the *Psyche* Odes—we listen to a very different voice. He is the seer now, and his utterances pierce and shake as few others in our whole range of song since Wordsworth declined from his best. And because this assertion is likely to be challenged, and certain to be misunderstood, I hasten to avow my conviction that Tennyson and Browning, Arnold, Swinburne —yes, and Meredith—are more excellent poets than Patmore. He was a learned theorist in metre, but neither a gifted singer nor an expert one. He could tell us most wisely that the language of poetry "should always seem to *feel,* though not to *suffer from,* the bonds of verse," and that metre never attains its noblest effects when it is altogether unproductive of "beautiful exorbitancies on the side of law." But these beautiful exorbitancies were not for him: his thoughts carried an exquisite sense of measure in speech and pause, but not their own music. His pace was ever the iambic. He called the metre of the *Odes* "catalectic," which may mean anything (except perhaps, "cataleptic") or nothing. "The system," says Mr. Champneys, "cannot be explained by analysis." In point of fact, there is no system at all, unless we call it system to break up the iambic line into irregular lengths according to the lift and fall of the poet's emotion. But music is something more than perfect measure; and though Patmore, in the *Odes,* paces, like Queen Elizabeth, "high and disposedly," he does not sing. Nor has he the steady, comprehensive poetical vision of the great ones I have named. He praises apprehension at the expense of comprehension, and upon apprehension he narrowed his aim. Yet now and then, beside his penetrating flashes, Browning's experimental psychology wears but a half-serious look, as of a clever game; Tennyson's *In Memoriam* keeps, indeed, its seriousness, but as the pathetic side of its inadequacy to its theme; while even the noble philosophies of Arnold and Meredith (though we return to them) are momentarily stunted in a glimpse of more tremendous heights.

The publication of the *Odes* (or, to give the volumes their titles, of *The Unknown Eros* and *Amelia*), in 1877–8, closed Patmore's career as a poet. Already he had moved from Heron's Ghyll to Hastings, and in 1891 he moved again to Lymington. To these later years, which he spent almost as a recluse, belong his prose writings, with their clear grasp of eternal principles and their indiscriminate ferocity against all contemporary hopes and strivings. His second wife died in 1880. In 1881 he married the lady who survives him, and by whose affectionate care much of the material of

Mr. Champneys' volumes has been collected. Patmore died on November 26, 1896, and was buried on December 1, robed in the habit of a tertiary of the Order of St. Francis.

A NOTE ON LONGINUS

I

"EVER and anon"—I quote from a book, *Essays of an Ex-Librarian,* by that good man the late Dr. Garnett, sometime of the British Museum—"ever and anon the world receives from some bright spirit a tiny golden book—some Longinus on the Sublime, or Mill on Liberty—to which nothing can be added and from which little can be taken away, in which the main outlines of the subject are perceived to have been traced by the hand of a master." "Such," goes on Dr. Garnett, "but for a few unfortunate infringements of literary decorum, is Matthew Arnold's trio of lectures *On Translating Homer*"—the subject of his Essay.

Well, I shall be among the very last to deny that Matthew Arnold's lectures *On Translating Homer* make a golden book, but I think more than a little of truth might be added to them and even something more than a little of error taken away: and in a lesser degree I can conceive this likely of Mill *On Liberty.* But of Longinus' famous little treatise Περὶ Ὕψους (commonly called Longinus *On the Sublime,* but with the meaning of the title better rendered, perhaps, in the sub-title invented by Leonard Welsted, who published a translation in 1712—*On the Sovereign Perfection of Writing*), Dr. Garnett's words are eminently true. Time has subtracted from it by destroying about a third of the MS., and the lacunae occur, not in a block, but dispersedly and irritatingly in the heart of the argument—*desunt duo folia, desunt sex folia, desunt duo folia.* Nevertheless, and notwithstanding that the discovery of a complete MS. would be one of the happiest literary troves conceivable; and again notwithstanding that the lost parts might, likely enough, contain references by which date and authorship could be fixed with some approach to certainty; the gaps do not *tantalise* us. We do not feel either that the argument, lacking them, is in any wise invalidated, or (I might even say) that their proper filling, while it commanded a pleasurable assent, would in any way astonish us or disconcert our opinion of the surviving two thirds. The treatise, in short, is so admirably rounded that we can guess the whole from the parts: and before I have done I shall have to point out to you that this very roundness and solidity of the Περὶ Ὕψους invites a damaging criticism.

II

Who wrote it: if his real name was Longinus; and, if it was, what particular Longinus and to what century he belonged; are questions admitting of a wide solution and as yet (as I have hinted) unsolved. It is no part of my purpose, and anyhow it would lie beyond my competence, to discuss with you the niceties of the evidence. They are dealt with, very fairly and lucidly, by Dr. W. Rhys Roberts [1] in an edition he prepared for the Cambridge University Press in 1899. I use a second edition of this, dated 1907, and I shall confine myself to a brief summary of the dispute *as it affects us.* The first

[1] Obiit 3 Oct. 1929. *Valde deflendus.* The news of his death reached me as I read the proof of this page.

edition of the treatise in print was issued at Basle in
1554 by Francis Robortello, who ascribed the authorship to "Dionysius Longinus"—Διονυσίου Λογγίνου ῥήτορος
Περὶ Ὕψους Βιβλίον—"the Book of Donysius Longinus
on the Sublime." In this ascription he was followed by
Paulus Manutius, who in the next year (1555) published
an edition in Venice. Now why it should have been at
once assumed (as apparently it was) that this "Dionysius
Longinus" was none other than the celebrated Cassius
Longinus, philosopher and adviser of the great Zenobia,
queen of Palmyra, upon whose capture and fall, in
278 A. D., he was put to death by the Emperor Aurelian,
I am unable to tell you, but so it was. Says Dr. Roberts:

The fashion thus set by the earliest editors became universal. Edition followed edition in quick succession, and
translations made the book known in almost every European
country. But in every issue of text or rendering Longinus
was assumed to be the author. It was the same with the
foremost critics and writers of France and of England.
Boileau was in this matter at one with the rest of the translators. His acquiescence in the general view was shared by
Fénelon, Rollin and Laharpe, and in England by Addison,
Hume, and Hurd. Pope, in a well-known passage, speaks of
the "bold Longinus" whose "own example strengthens all his
laws." And even the severely scientific Gibbon refers, with
some hesitation possibly in the choice of the adjective but
with no hesitation in the choice of the name, to the "sublime
Longinus."

It may be dull of me, but I do not understand what
Dr. Roberts intends by the phrase "with some hesitation
possibly in the choice of the adjective": for, in the
passage alluded to, Gibbon plainly uses the epithet to
identify his author; by "the sublime Longinus" indi-

cating that Longinus who wrote *On the Sublime,* even as we might say "the self-helpful Smiles"; "the seasonable James Thomson" to indicate that we are talking about the author of *The Seasons* and not of that other James Thomson who wrote *The City of Dreadful Night.* Moreover, Gibbon proceeds in the very same paragraph to remove (at unawares) all doubt on this point by backing his allusion to "sublime Longinus" with a quotation from the famous 44th Chapter of the Περὶ Ὕψους and even adds a footnote containing Pope's line already quoted:

His own example strengthens all his laws.

The fact is, neither Gibbon nor any one else in Gibbon's day had a suspicion that the famous Longinus of the third century—Zenobia's Longinus—was not the author of our treatise. That doubt first arose in 1808 with the discovery by the Italian scholar Amati that a Vatican MS. contained the ascription Διονυσίου ἢ Λογγίνου περὶ ὕψους —"Dionysius *or* Longinus *On the Sublime.*" On top of this discovery came another: that a tenth-century codex at Paris, admitted to be the very best extant, gave the same alternative—"Dionysius or Longinus." On top of this, again, more trouble—a manuscript at Florence was reported as bearing on its cover ἀνωνύμου περὶ ὕψους— that is, *"On the Sublime.* Author Unknown." There were minor discoveries, too, more or less coincident: but (to cut the story short) scholars have tended more and more, during the hundred-odd years since Amati's discovery, to doubt—even to deny—that Zenobia's Longinus wrote our treatise, and to hold that it really belongs to the first, not the third, century after Christ.

III

"Dionysius *or* Longinus"—I shall make here, **very** diffidently, one small contribution to the dispute. The alternative name Dionysius, at once, of course, suggested Dionysius of Halicarnassus who set up in Rome as a rhetorician and writer about 30 B.C. and composed among more ambitious works (including a *History of Rome*) three literary letters which, in translation—also by Dr. Roberts—those of you who are reading in Literary Criticism for the English Tripos will find worth your perusal, being (as the saying is) "full of meat." But that their author was also the author of this treatise *On the Sublime* I cannot bring myself to believe; for several reasons, among which I shall only specify his repeated strictures on Plato and their variance, not only in view but in *quality of mind,* from the noble sympathy of Longinus (as for handiness, and begging no question, I shall continue to call him). A man may change his opinion concerning an author : most of you, if the gods grant you years and intellectual growth, will change your opinions concerning many authors. A man, for example, may begin by cursing and end by blessing George Meredith, or Thomas Hardy, or Browning, or Svnge, or Bergson or James, or anyone you like. A man may repeat his cursing times and again, and yet turn to bless at the last or *vice versâ.* A man may in repeated strictures so mitigate them by allowance of praise (and Dionysius does *that*) as to get his final conversion mistaken for a natural process. But he is still converted *in opinion.* He cannot change his *quality of mind.* Now the quality of mind in one who could fasten (as Dionysius did) upon Plato's *Menexenus* and take that neat piece of irony—so playful with a touch of seriousness—and possibly not Plato's at all, by the way—and trounce that for serious Plato—has an obtuseness not to be reconciled with anything in the Περὶ Ὕψους. Some five years ago, in a lecture on *Patriotism in English Literature,* I gave you a brief account of this *Menexenus,* a supposed funeral oration, carefully absurd in its dates, obviously travestied from Pericles' famous funeral speech as conjectured for him by Thucydides. You might as well treat it solemnly as take Mr. Max Beerbohm's Savonarola Jones's *Savonarola* solemnly for his notion of serious writing. And Plato (or whoever it was) makes Socrates put this oration "on our honoured dead" into the mouth of—Aspasia of all people. Which is just as if we should put a like oration into the mouth of Mrs. . . . well, into the mouth of the latest lady to make play among public events too high for her conception either of them, or innumerous private sorrows (caused by them) and all far too deep for any understanding that she can ever reach. That the somewhat stupid man who took the *Menexenus* so is our Longinus, I, for one, find incredible. Merely to be able to take it so postulates for me a greater deficiency of tact than we can accuse upon the author of our treatise.

IV

But now to come to what concerns *us.* Whoever wrote the treatise, it exercised, for almost two centuries, an amazing authority over our critics and practitioners in literature. In the whole period of that influence I dare say you can choose no figures more eminent than John Dryden and Edmund Burke. Let us see what Longinus *On the Sublime* meant to these two.

Dryden, who is constantly quoting him in his Prefaces,

says downright in his *Apology for Heroic Poetry* that
Longinus "was undoubtedly, after Aristotle, the greatest
critic among the Greeks"; and no one who reads
Dryden's Prefaces in comparison with the Περὶ Ὕψους can
doubt for a moment either that he had his Longinus
fairly by heart—as he had his *Poetics*—or that he meant
what he said. With Burke (though one might quote at
large from his tractate *On the Sublime and Beautiful*)
let us take another way and, choosing a well-known
passage, show how closely and carefully he practises upon
the book that, we know, gave him his theory. It is commonplace to say that the educated Roman was immensely
concerned with Rhetoric. He, above all other men that
have lived, dealt out laws to the world, inventing them
and afterwards refining them by interpretation. Greece
in the story of our Civilisation stands for Literature:
Rome for Law. The Roman was no natural poet: he
had a lawyer's, a pleader's attitude towards the whole
literary business: and his literary instructors—adaptable
Greeks for the most part, having twice his *wits* at the
least—had, whether they liked it or not, to turn rhetori-
cians and teach literature in terms of rhetoric. (As descendants of the sophists they bent themselves to the
yoke easily enough, no doubt.) Now, whoever our
Longinus was, he makes it plain to us that he delighted
in poetry but that his "job"—so to say—was the rhetoric
his employers demanded. You may place him chrono-
logically where you please; in the first or in the third
century. However you place him, his models are, in the
main, men who were long ago dead when he wrote and
I at any rate see him as a man harking wistfully back
to them, trying to yoke them up to the rhetorical business—so different then and always from the business of
poetry—that he has perforce in hand. Lucretius has

gone, and Virgil has followed, and Cicero in turn is gone.

Now Longinus has a great deal to say in his treatise about an excellent help to sublimity, termed by him Amplification. "This figure," he says, "is employed when the narrative or the course of a forensic argument admits, from section to section, of many starting-points and many pauses, and elevated expressions follow, one after another, in an unbroken succession and in an ascending order." (For further embroidery on this definition I refer you to Chapters XI and XII of Longinus' treatise.) With that in your minds I beg you to listen to the following famous passage from Burke and to note, step by step, its deliberate amplification. Burke has been finding reasons for the intractable spirit of the American Colonists and he comes at length to this:

The last cause of this disobedient spirit in the Colonies is hardly less powerful than the rest, as it is not merely moral, but laid deep in the natural constitution of things. Three thousand miles of ocean lie between you and them. No contrivance can prevent the effect of this distance in weakening government. Seas roll, and months pass, between the order and the execution; and the want of a speedy explanation of a single point is enough to defeat a whole system. You have, indeed, winged ministers of vengeance, who carry your bolts in their pounces to the remotest verge of the sea. But there a power steps in, that limits the arrogance of raging passions and furious elements, and says, *So far shalt thou go, and no farther*. Who are you, that you should fret and rage, and bite the chains of Nature? Nothing worse happens to you than does to all nations who have extensive Empire: and it happens in all the forms into which Empire can be thrown. In large bodies, the circulation of power must be less vigorous at the extremities. Nature has said it. The Turk cannot govern Ægypt, and Arabia, and Curdistan as he governs

Thrace; nor has he the same dominion in Crimea and Algiers, which he has in Brusa and Smyrna. Despotism itself is obliged to truck and huckster. The Sultan gets such obedience as he can. He governs with a loose rein that he may govern at all; and the whole of the force and vigour of his authority in his centre is derived from a prudent relaxation in all his borders. Spain, in her provinces, is perhaps not so well obeyed as you are in yours. She complies too; she submits; she watches times. This is the immutable condition, the eternal Law, of extensive and detached Empire.

V

Now that, in its Asiatic style, is fine prose for its purpose, that purpose being Oratory; but it is "amplifying" all the while, and it amplifies one very simple proposition—that a large Empire is less wieldy than a small one. To have written just that (in some better brevity of wording of course), and to have left it at that, would have suited Burke's purpose may be as well, may be much better, had he been writing for print. He could have found one arresting phrase for this very simple thought and left it on the page (underlined, that is to say italicised, if he chose) for the reader to pause upon and ponder. But the orator works for the moment and must often contrive his effect, his necessary emphasis, by artificially prolonging the moment: for the spoken word vanishes with its utterance: the air receives it and it is nowhere, with no trace but in the hearer's memory—to strengthen which, therefore, the speaker employs all his art. I seem to remember a majestic utterance by the late Mr. Herbert Spencer (I am sorry that I cannot guarantee to quote it *verbatim;* but hope I do it no serious damage; for Mr. Spencer's lips did not drop linked jewels, though he pardonably supposed and publicly maintained, or came near to maintaining, that they did)—shall I then say rather, that I dimly recall an utterance of his to this effect: "It is only by frequent and varied iteration that unfamiliar truths can be impressed upon reluctant minds." Well, you see that even Herbert Spencer allows even of the written, the printed word, the necessity of *varying* our iteration. For the spoken word this necessity is clearly absolute, since no assembly would tolerate an orator who for emphasis said the same thing ten times over in identical terms. You see, then, the purpose of *amplification* and its use in oratory. As Longinus puts it, amplification is not proof, but gives strength to the argument by dwelling on it and aggregating upon it a number of instances, topics and illustrations. But you see also that it does nothing like the same service to the printed page; that the prose *writer* may all too easily find it a besetting temptation, and his reader an irritating nuisance. And, as it happens, I can fortify this from the history of that very passage of Burke's which I have quoted. Lord Brougham, as you know, was an orator, and a somewhat florid one. Moreover those acquainted with the works of both will bear me out that Brougham never hesitated, at a pinch, to borrow a thought or a similitude from Burke. As it happens, I say, Brougham found it convenient to borrow the gist of this very thought of Burke's for an early tract which he entitled *An Inquiry into the Colonial Policy of the European Powers* (you note, the borrowing was operated *in pari materia*), and this is the form he gives it:

In all the despotisms of the East it has been observed that, the farther any part of the empire is removed from the

capital, the more do its inhabitants enjoy some sort of rights
and privileges; the more inefficacious is the power of the
monarch; and the more feeble and easily decayed is the
organisation of the government.

The late Mr. E. J. Payne of Lincoln's Inn, barrister-at-
law, who hid away in a couple of schoolbooks two of
the ripest, most learned, disquisitions ever written upon
Burke, sets this passage of Brougham's alongside a few
sentences of Burke's to illustrate the value of concrete terms in energising style. "The Turk cannot
govern Egypt and Arabia and Curdistan as he governs
Thrace. . . . The Sultan gets such obedience as he
can. He governs with a loose rein, that he may govern
at all": and Heaven forbid my saying a word against
that. You know on the contrary that I am always
preaching this very sermon: that I rate you in private
when you talk about poetry in the abstract and not about
the actual *Hamlet,* the actual *Paradise Lost,* the actual
Ode to a Nightingale: that I thump the desk until its
very bowels acknowledge that it is a desk of wood, of
this length and that width, and not an educational
accessory: that all my teaching goes to reinforce, or
strives to reinforce Mr. Payne's praise of concrete
writing. "This particularising style," he says, "is of the
essence of poetry; and in prose it is impossible not to be
struck with the energy it produces." Nevertheless I use
the parallel with another purpose than Mr. Payne's: and
I say that, flaccid as is Brougham in comparison with
Burke, he *has* a sense that for written prose Burke's
rhetorical amplifying is inappropriate, and would sur-
charge the reader's patience; and that though the execution is mean and impoverishes the original of all its

imaginative splendour, yet somehow the instinct to re-
duce it was right, while the knack was missing.

VI

I have dwelt on this passage of Burke's for two
reasons. In the first place it exhibits—as I could quote
many another to exhibit—Burke in the act of deliberately amplifying upon a rule laid down by Longinus. I
make no doubt at all that, if tackled on it, Burke would
have retorted by quoting Longinus' precept of amplification, and would have been immensely surprised to find
Longinus not accepted by us as, if not an absolute, at
least a most puissant authority. It would have been one
of the shocks of his life, as we say. And yet, within a
very few years of Burke's death, this puissant authority
of Longinus had become the palest of shadows. During
the seventeenth and eighteenth centuries he holds sway—
increasing sway—over the minds of all men who think
about literature. Then all of a sudden, as it were, he
fades almost quite away, and during the nineteenth
century critics seldom concern themselves to quote him.
I shall attempt to give a reason or two for this by-and-
by.

But, secondly, I have dwelt upon this specimen of
Burke's amplifying (in obedience to Longinus) because
it indicates a special bias, as I may call it, for which we
must be constantly on the watch—against which we
must be steadily on our guard as we read him or
Quintilian or any ancient critic later than Aristotle for
that study of the History of Literary Criticism which
our English Tripos includes. Just as with any one of
our Elizabethan critics—with Sidney for example—we
must be prepared at any moment to find him commend-

ing Poetry, and with unction, for its moral purpose,
disguising the real reason why it is admirable and he
adores it, under a pretence that it and he are preoccupied
with conscious moral edification—so and no less closely
should we watch these ancients for the *professionising
touch*. For keep it clear to yourselves that these men
were all teachers of rhetoric and earned their living by
it. As I said, a while back, the chief intellectual aim of
Rome was to make law for the world, and to interpret,
to elucidate that law. For that pre-eminently she trained
her best minds: and rhetoric, being, as you know, alike
the weapon of the senator in legislative discussion and
of the advocate in courts which apply the law enacted,
for that she hired her Greek and other foreign instructors. The logical traffic, the dialectic, of the old
Greek sophists was (I repeat) mere play—or, as we
may put it, intellectual chat—compared with the strict
professional purpose of these men: whose criticism
quite naturally becomes

<blockquote>subdued
To what it works in, like the dyer's hand</blockquote>

—so that, when their natural love of poetry asserts
itself, as again and again it does, we may find them at
any moment recalled as if by a bell in the servants' hall
to the duty for which they were engaged.

VII

It is Longinus' great merit for us—whatever it may
have seemed to his clients (including a possible Zenobia)
—that his book never really confuses flash rhetoric or
artifice with genuine sublimity, which indeed he defines
as "a certain distinction and excellence of expression."

"As all lights," he says, "are extinguished in the glare of the sun, so do all the artifices of rhetoric fade from view in the pervading splendour of sublimity." Again, after enumerating five principal sources of elevated language —great conception, vehement passion (these two innate) ; the gift of translating thought and expression into figurative imagery, noble diction, dignified composition (these three in part the product of art)—he loses no time in assuring us that, of these, the power of great conception (which comes of natural elevation of mind— τὸ μεγαλοφυές) ranks first and foremost of all. For (says he) "as I have written elsewhere, *Sublimity is the echo of a great soul.* . . . The truly eloquent must be free from low and ignoble thoughts: since it is not possible that men with mean and servile ideas and aims prevailing throughout their lives should produce what is admirable and worthy of immortality. Great accents we expect to fall from the lips of those whose thoughts are weighty: and things *in excelsis* make a province for lofty minds."

Knowing this, and aware of it so well that even in the few by-ways of his tract this one truth never deserts his side, Longinus is equally sure that (whatever may be said for Rhetoric) Poetry is the right medium in which the greatest of souls reveal and express themselves: and his criticism of any poetical passage may equally be relied on for enjoyment (for gusto, if you will) and for sure judgment. He is not one of your finality men. For his age—and whether we decide to assign him to the first century or to the third—he is often quite curiously modern. To him the world owes, if by accident, an eternal debt for having preserved to it in this treatise, an exquisite lyric of Sappho's, even as it owns a like to Dionysius for having embalmed in his *De Compositione,* as it is called, that other marvellous thing of hers,

Ποικιλόθρον᾽, ἀθάνατ᾽ ᾽Αφροδίτα . . .

But how "modern" must have appeared, to any contemporary reader, this citation from the Pentateuch of the right way to make a God speak—

Similarly the legislator of the Jews, no ordinary man, having formed and expressed a worthy conception of the Godhead, writes at the very beginning of his Laws, *God said* —What? *"Let there be light" and there was light: "let there be land" and there was land.*

VIII

I have said that after exerting, for the greater part of the seventeenth and eighteenth centuries, an unquestioned authority upon European criticism, Longinus *On the Sublime* seems almost suddenly and without a word to abdicate all hold on men's veneration, even on their interest. He is not disproved—for that matter, he cannot be disproved. Nobody attempts the ungracious task of dismissing him. Quite as though sublimity had, on some unnoted reposeful moment in the world's active consciousness, turned into a Snark, Longinus softly and suddenly vanishes away. Nineteenth-century critics seldom vex a spirit which has (as if warned by a cock-crow inaudible save to itself) turned and gone back to its rest, unassisted by anyone.

So you see that even the History of Literary Criticism may haply contain its ghost-story.

Now since, so far as my reading goes, no one has seriously attempted to account for this strange and swift *dis*apparition—and since, as an unexplained phenomenon, it deserves and is even important enough to demand our attention—I shall conclude by attempting an explanation, offering two reasons which have occurred to me, and offering the less convincing first, though I believe them both to be cogent.

In the first place, then, no one can read this short treatise without noting that it is the utterance of a man in despair with his age, and particularly in despair with it over its loss of Liberty. In a previous lecture I quoted to you a fine passage from his last chapter which can scarcely, in these times, be too often repeated.

"It remains" [he says] "to clear up, my dear Terentianus, a question which a certain philosopher has recently mooted. I wonder," he says, "as no doubt do many others, how it happens that in our time there are men who have the gift of persuasion to the utmost extent, and are well fitted for public life, and are keen and ready, and particularly rich in all the charms of language, yet there no longer arise really lofty and transcendent natures unless it be quite peradventure. So great and world-wide a dearth of high utterance attends our age. Can it be," he continued, "we are to accept the common cant that democracy is the nursing mother of genius, and that great men of letters flourish and die with it? For freedom, they say, has the power to cherish and encourage magnanimous minds, and with it is disseminated eager mutual rivalry and the emulous thirst to excel. Moreover, by the prizes open under a popular government, the mental faculties of orators are perpetually practised and whetted, and, as it were, rubbed bright, so that they shine free as the State itself. Whereas to-day," he went on, "we seem to have learnt as an infant-lesson that servitude is the law of life; being all wrapped, while our thoughts are yet young and tender, in observances and customs as in swaddling clothes, bound without access to that fairest and most fertile source of man's speech (I mean Freedom) so that we are turned out in no other guise than that of servile flatterers. And servitude (it has been well said) though it be even righteous, is the cage of the soul and a public prison-house."

But I answered him thus.—"It is easy, my good sir, and characteristic of human nature, to gird at the age in which one lives. Yet consider whether it may not be true that it is less the world's peace that ruins noble nature than this war illimitable which holds our aspirations in its fist, and occupies our age with passions as with troops that utterly plunder and harry it. The love of money and the love of pleasure enslave us, or rather, as one may say, drown us body and soul in their depths. For vast and unchecked wealth marches with lust of pleasure for comrade, and when one opens the gate of house or city, the other at once enters and abides. And in time these two build nests in the hearts of men, and quickly rear a progeny only too legitimate: and the ruin within the man is gradually consummated as the sublimities of his soul wither away and fade, and in ecstatic contemplation of our mortal parts we omit to exalt, and come to neglect in nonchalance, that within us which is immortal."

Now I suggest that a passage like that—all too true of the time when it was written (the first or the third century) would to one eighteenth-century man—I am thinking of Burke—carry a genuine and delightful antiquarian interest: for Burke seriously believed that he *was* free; by the inestimable mercy of the Great Revolution and the accession of William of Orange a free citizen of a free country senatorially ruled; he himself being one of the Senate, though on the Opposition side of the Lower House. But when the Romantics came along, they blew upon the convention in which Burke had his being, and lo! it was putrid. They knew that, alike under Toryism and under Whiggery, our people lived under a convention and were not free. So—and this is the point—these Romantics had no use at all for the delicate regretful consent of Longinus in the decadence of his age: for these men were fighters. You may misprise the nineteenth century and easily just now, as every age in turn despises its immediate predecessor: but (I warn you) you will despise it to your lasting cost: for it was above all centuries the century in which men—Shelley and Bolivar and Garibaldi let me name—lived for that mysterious but most holy thing, the Idea of Liberty. Such men made their age; and that age, being out to win, had no use for regrets which involved acceptance, or for criticism which, disgusted with the house, sought back for its rest to a time long since past.

IX

And so I come to my second reason for the more-than-partial eclipse, during the nineteenth century, of this admirable Essay. For the preceding age—of scholars and gentlemen—it was admirably adapted. It did not play with authors that were new even in Longinus' time. It took any author from Homer to Cicero and said the final word. It is all exquisitely mellow, and seldom wrong. And I desire you who are young and impatient to remind yourselves that to taste old wine and old authors judiciously is one of the few vivid joys left to men of—shall we say?—my time of life. Sooner or later I promise you of Longinus, as has been said of Montaigne, you will be glad to cross your knees and lift your wine to the light in his panelled library.

Still—and thank Heaven!—the mischief with the final word in this unstable world is precisely that it *is* final; whereas in criticism of literature, which is (however it may disguise itself) in the end criticism of life, no word can ever be final: and the more it seems or affects to be final the less it can be true. I remember a character in one of Meredith's novels—probably Dr. Middleton— who lets fall at the dinner-table a remark at once apt, striking, profoundly true, and in every way admirable save that it instantly killed the conversation. Now that, or something like that, is the trouble with Longinus and his ripe judgment. In my experience—which some of you have the fate to share—any sentence of Aristotle's *Poetics* may start, on any instant, some seminal discussion to which nothing but the clock can put an end. But when Longinus has spoken, he has spoken: nothing remains to be said: and we feel that the business is somehow in its perfection perfectly wrong; because, as a fact, literature must move with life as a condition of its own being. There is no final word on it, nor ever can be.

ON READING FOR THE ENGLISH TRIPOS

I

IT was suggested to me, Gentlemen, at the end of last term that—our English Tripos at Cambridge being at once a new thing in the sense that an infant is new, and in its idea something of an innovation upon the pattern adopted by other Universities in their Schools of English Language and Literature—a lecture might not be wasted which gave you some practical suggestions and hints *how to read for it*. That is my theme this morning; and I attempt it the more cheerfully, believing that you, to whose age belong hope and imagination, will divine, under some plain words of advice, what certain men were driving at who designed your English Tripos—yes and may yet ask leave of the Senate to improve it, seeing that none of us ever pretended to a brain like Olympian Jove's, out of which (as you will remember) the goddess of wisdom sprang to birth at full stature dressed in complete armour. Our enemies will, of course, call this "tinkering"; but men tinker a leaky vessel, not one that is full—as in two years ours has become—to overflowing. They then, if they have sense in their heads, use it to design an ampler one.

II

Our notion, then, was of an English School which should train men of your age in understanding, rather than test them in memorised information; should teach you less to hoard facts than to deal with them, to sift out what you accumulate and even to accumulate with economy: so that (as I put it in my very first lecture up here) "the man we are proud to send forth from our School will be remarkable less for anything he can produce from his wallet and exhibit for knowledge than for being something, and that something a man of unmistakable breeding, whose judgment can be trusted to choose the better and reject the worse." For a first piece of advice then, get it out of your minds that we require omniscience of you, even in the limited field of English Literature: since even in that limited field omniscience will cost at least a scholar's life-time, and you have but two academic years between now and the day when we —ourselves by no means omniscient—come to examine you.

We do not require omniscience, then. But I hasten to add that we require some knowledge; even a considerable amount of knowledge: and to warn anyone who tells himself, or allows anyone to persuade him, that our English Tripos here is a "soft option," to be attempted on a year's reading, will be backing his self-conceit. Against a man of something like genius who has already taken a high class in the First Part of the Classical Tripos the odds will run lower than against one less generously endowed by nature and by training less happily prepared. But they will yet be formidable.

III

I want to impress *that* upon you at the very start, lest you should lay out your time up here on a bet against disappointment: and I shall fetch you the "why" of it—*fas est ab hoste doceri*—out of the mental process of those who will go on ingeminating "soft option" until they "cease upon the midnight with no pain," bequeathing to you the legacy of your own third-class ticket. I want you to see just how far these testators have reasonable warrant that you may the better see how finally they escape their own notice being mistaken.

In the first place, then, our English Tripos is largely if not mainly concerned with the study of literature—which I may for the moment define roughly as "memorable speech." [I avoid limiting it to *written* speech, reminding you that the *Iliad*—to which no one refuses the name of "literature"—was likely enough composed and chanted by a man, or by a number of men, who could not, as we say, put pen to paper.] Now literature differs from the sister arts of painting, sculpture, dancing, music, in this among other ways, and in this most eminently, that it works in a familiar medium—speech —which we are all using for the most ordinary purposes the day through, every day of our lives, and always with a purpose, if less ambitious, yet not different in kind from that of the poet or the orator. When, for example, you or I order a herring for breakfast, we use language which, if not designed to be eternally memorable and outlast the pyramids, we hope to endure in somebody's memory until the herring appears. We neither paint the fish, nor engrave its image on stone, nor indicate its attributes by motions of the body, nor suggest them upon the pipe or lute or full organ or other instrument of music. We express our desire for a herring by precisely the same medium as Richard the Third at Bosworth expresses his desire for a horse, or a Hamlet or a Shelley their craving that this too-too solid flesh would melt and make way for a more rarefied, a more etherial scheme of things.

Let me press home this point in the words of one of the wisest among the sons of Cambridge of the last generation—Henry Sidgwick; a teacher who himself exemplified in his time many of the finest virtues of this place; candour and intellectual courage, a disinterested love of truth, a modesty in presenting it; above all, a charity so large for the opinions of others and so quick a sensibility for their feelings that it did better than repress—it *forgot*—all instinct of self-assertion. Such was Henry Sidgwick as I had the honour to know him, and no man known to me was ever less afraid of the obvious or less concerned with his own reputation in readiness to state the obvious, if need were or it happened to be important.

Literature [he says] alone of the arts shows us the highest excellence in a kind of productive activity in which we all take some part. We do not only, as the *bourgeois* of comedy puts it, talk prose all our life without knowing it, but when eager to communicate experiences, ideas, and feelings, we talk or write as expressive prose as we can; thus the *technique* of the great artists in words is only the glorified form of a skill that we all seek, and in some humble degree learn to exercise.

Now that, I say, may seem to you a truism. But, obvious or not, it conditions all enquiry into the likeness or unlikeness of literature and the sister arts, and, obvious or not, it has escaped the notice of a number—I should say the majority—of enquirers. For example, it leads us straight on to what Sidgwick calls the *altruism* of literature compared with the other arts: of which she is at once queen and *serva servarum,* using some of her happiest hours in teaching us of her sisters' charms —of painting, sculpture, architecture, music—as when

Ruskin discourses on Turner or the Stones of Venice, Pater on Giotto, on Leonardo da Vinci, or—to name a particular debt of my own—Richard Jefferies on that lovely neglected torso, the Venus Accroupie of the Louvre.

But I digress and must recur to my point.

Our critics, then, perceiving that we deal with literature, the *technique* of which, at its best, is but "the glorified form of a skill that we all seek, and in some humble way learn to exercise," naturally incline next to ask, if we provide the requisite difficulty, the "mental gymnastic," as they sometimes term it—by setting up the obstacle of some foreign language, hard to master; the obstacle of Greek for instance, or of literary French. When we answer "No: the language is our mother tongue, already for utility learnt by us all in our nurseries," they as naturally reply "It is—it must be, then— what we suspected it for: a soft option."

And they would be right were we content with a standard even nearly equivalent to that which the French Tripos demands in French or the Classical Tripos in Greek: or with any comparable standard.

But we are not. We recognise that the student of any foreign language has to surmount a hill on the summit of which our English student has already arrived to view the plain below him as Cortez overlooked Mexico. And therefore of set purpose we have made our English Tripos a *difficult* school. Why, the old objection of our opponents, while we were making it, lay just here— that it was designed for first-class men: to which we answered cheerfully, "Yes: and not only a school for first-class men, but one in which (please Heaven) it will be hard enough for one of these to get a first class." We deliberately set this standard: and those who tell you that a high standard is impossible in a subject so easy by nature are making an assumption, laying down an axiom, the ground of which we challenge. Let me put it in this way. I imagine that, as well-intentioned men, these *a priori* critics would be happy indeed if we and they together could in modern England recreate that spirit of intellectual curiosity, that thirst for truth, that passion for beauty governed by temperance, that energy of experiment in art, politics, poetry and the comely adornments of life, civic, social, domestic, and all that efflorescence of the human mind which broke over Hellas in the fifth century B.C., and especially over Athens, even as the writer of the old Homeric hymn saw Apollo pass up Cnidos and

> Delos broke in gold
> Beneath his feet, as on a mountain-side
> Sudden, in Spring, a bush is glorified
> And canopied with blossom manifold.

"Another Athens shall arise"—? Well, if our friends share this hope, let them consider the astonishing fact that all these marvels were achieved by a race which knew its own language *and that language alone*.

IV

Yes, we require a high standard. I repeat, we do *not* require omniscience; should, indeed, run away from it. At the end of your reading you will be sent six papers, each to be answered in three hours, and each comprising some seventeen to twenty questions. Of these in each paper you will be asked to answer five and discouraged from selecting more than five. For I should tell you that our effort is to discover what you know, not to detect what you don't: and I pray you, once for all, to get that into your heads. The papers, whether on a period or a subject, are set with an earnest desire that you should do yourselves justice. And I put it to you that a paper of seventeen to twenty questions out of which you select five is a paper in which we supply the quantity out of which you disengage what quality, if any, happens to be in you.

More than this—If you are naturally a slow writer —and I have known many who cannot do their best against time, some even who are handicapped by their very conscientiousness in choosing the right word [please take this from one who has, at any time these thirty years and more, found the construction of English sentences a confounded nuisance]—you may still improve your class, if it be in doubt, by sending in a sample of what you can write, at leisure, on any subject of your own choice. *The Student's Handbook* tells you this, in words explicit enough: but I would have you get into your minds one pleasant property of these extraneous compositions (as I will call them); that while they have the chance to improve your class by much or by little, they cannot by any chance do it harm: for by a rule of our Examination they either count for good or are ignored.

V

But to turn to the actual test of the Schools and your reading for that. . . . When an undergraduate comes to me (and many do) at the end of a May term, announces his intention to read for the English Tripos, and asks with what preparatory study he should beguile

the Long Vacation which stands between him and his
champing enthusiasm for the lecture-room, I suggest
as a rule that he start by reading as many of the works
of Shakespeare as he can find leisure for: reading each
play twice; the first time at long breath, without interruption, or pausing only to consult a note or a glossary
when the meaning of a passage quite defeats him: the
second time *with* a commentary, marking the passages
which he had overpassed, thinking them easy enough,
but now finds to hold an unsuspected significance. That
this simple counsel may be mistaken for silliness I infer
from the disappointed drop of the jaw with which so
many have received it. But I believe it to be a little
less silly than it looks: since not only is Shakespeare one
of your compulsory subjects but—and this is very much
more to the point—with all Shakespeare's faults, in
reading him you are living on terms with greatness.
Even when engaged in separating his good from his
bad (and, as his plays have reached us, he can be exceedingly bad at times) you are dealing with noble stuff
of the mind, familiarising yourselves with largeness, and
so (albeit for the moment unconsciously) learning what
English Literature *can* be: so, too (albeit unconsciously),
learning what the first-rate truly is, and to discern what
marks it above the second-, third- and fourth-rate.

VI

My next advice is that you get a general *conspectus* of
the "periods" into which for convenience we parcel out
our "periods" of Literature: in Saintsbury's or Lang's
Short Histories or Jusserand, for instance: concurrently
running through some book which connects our English
stream (mighty, but yet a confluent) with the grand flood

of European Literature: and for this you will find such books as Professor W. P. Ker's *The Dark Ages,* Dr. Coulton's books, Madame Duclaux' *The End of the Middle Ages:* with (for your "Special Period") Professor Oliver Elton's *Surveys.* And then there is always *The Cambridge History of English Literature,* of course —any volume of it—to stop a hole and keep the wind away.

I name these works very carelessly: they are good, but others will do: for you should use them—not to consign dates, names, details, to your memory, but to acquire a general sense of the relativities of A, B and C in any given period; how the second- and third-rate stood to the best, what in that A, B and C were consentaneously driving at and how they helped one another. So long as your reading here instructs you to fasten on the great authors: Chaucer and Henryson; Spenser, Marlowe, Donne; Bacon, Milton, Dryden, Pope, Samuel Johnson, Burke; Coleridge, Wordsworth, Keats, Byron, Shelley; Dickens, Browning, Carlyle—to name but a few—these books will do you their best service. Nor am I for a moment afraid of the charge of counselling shallowness in advising you to treat all such mere handbooks just as they serve your purpose and, beyond that, as cavalierly as you will. For they are all books *about* literature: and I tell you frankly that any amount of knowledge *about* literature is in the idea of this Tripos worthless as compared with a true, if limited, understanding of *what literature is about.*

VII

Thus far, then, for preliminary counsel. But you come up here in October, and want—or let me put it more hesitatingly—you think it advisable to attend lectures.

Well, if you will, you will: but do not attend too many. I somewhat artfully introduced, just now, the name of Henry Sidgwick—not, believe me, topically, because he was the first to bring women to Cambridge (I hope you bear his memory no grudge for that)—but simply as a prelude to some wise words of his upon Lectures. He was sound enough anyhow upon that subject. He held that we give too many lectures here at Cambridge: and on some few years' experience I can at any rate agree that you *attend* too many lectures; consoling you—on the polite supposition that we are out of earshot and beyond range of eavesdroppers— with the assurance that, while you attend too many, the Women Students attend *far* too many.

He set out this opinion in *A Lecture against Lecturing,* which you may find in a posthumous volume of *Miscellaneous Essays and Addresses.* I wish this one could be reprinted separately and cheaply (since the volume is not easy to procure), made accessible to all of you, and imposed as an article of study upon all Supervisors of Studies. As it is, I content myself with culling a few extracts. After stating the customary notion of a lecture—that the teacher and his class should be brought together in a room at a certain hour on an advertised day, and that the teacher should expound his subject in a series of discourses varying from forty-five to sixty minutes in duration [and I have sat

here, where men sit and hear each other groan

on occasions when even that generous limit has been exceeded]—he proceeds:

This is the traditional, time-honoured, almost universal practice of University Professors, ordinary or extraordinary, in the countries that share European civilisation: it is supported by an overwhelming consensus of opinion and practice, and most persons with whom I have spoken on the subject hardly seem able to conceive it as either needing or admitting fundamental alteration.   I do not mean that what I have described is universally held to constitute the whole of a professor's educational function.   In England, at any rate, it is generally thought that academic teaching, to be effective, must include some kind of exercises written by the student and looked over by the teacher, and some kind of ˉoral communication between the two, in the way of question and answer.   In Germany[1], however, the instrument of academic instruction is—in most departments of study . . . simply the lecture; and even in England it is commonly thought to be the main if not the sole educational business of a professor to expound his subject in a course of lectures.

This view appeared to Sidgwick radically erroneous. He goes on—

I regard the ordinary expository lecture—in most subjects, and so far as the most intelligent class of students are con- cerned—as an antiquated survival: a relic of the times before the printing press was invented; maintained partly by habit and the prestige of ancient tradition, partly by the difficulty . . . of finding a right substitute for it.

To defend this heresy he first carefully limits it "in order not to present too broad a front to an orthodox opponent": and he therefore excepts from his criticism

lectures of which the method is dialectic and not simply expository; and lectures on science or art, in which the

[1] This was written in 1890.

exhibition of experiments or specimens forms an essential part of the plan of instruction: and again lectures on art or literature, so far as they aim at emotional and aesthetic, not purely intellectual effects. . . .

I still wait anxiously, Gentlemen, for my own discharge. It comes in the following words—

—and lectures on any subject whatever that are intended to stimulate interest rather than convey information.

I can confidently claim that anything I have ever said from this desk may claim exemption on *that* ground: and am cheered, if not at heart convinced, by his further assurance that "for all these purposes the use of lectures will increase rather than diminish as civilisation progresses."

VIII

Well, well . . . I have not time even to condense the full argument: but it backs up a word I seem to remember saying from this place—no doubt somewhat too vivaciously—some time ago: that the Universities of Oxford and Cambridge have never yet thoroughly realised that Koster, Fust, or Gutenberg (whichever it was) invented the art of printing some time in the fifteenth century, or that our Caxton imported it, setting up his stall in Westminster. I was not thinking, nor was Sidgwick, on the one hand of the pass-men on whom compulsion into a lecture room no doubt increases their chance of imbibing knowledge, since it is difficult to find amusement during a lecture which distract one's attention completely from the lecturer. "Although," says he, "I have known instances in which the difficulty has been overcome by patient ingenuity." Nor on the other hand am I thinking of the lecturer aimed at by the bard (but he was, to be sure, an Oxford one) who sang :

> When Autumn's leaves denude the grove,
> 　I seek my Lecture, where it lurks
> 'Mid the unpublished portion of
> 　My works,
>
> And ponder, while its sheets I scan,
> 　How many years away have slipt
> Since first I penn'd that ancient man-
> 　uscript.
>
> I know thee well—nor can mistake
> 　The old accustomed pencil-stroke
> Denoting when I mostly make
> 　A joke,—
>
> Or where coy brackets signify
> 　Those echoes faint of ancient wit
> Which, if a lady's present, I
> 　Omit.
>
> Though Truth enlarge her widening range,
> 　And Knowledge be with time increased,
> While thou, my Lecture! dost not change
> 　The least,
>
> But fixed immutable amidst
> 　The advent of a newer lore
> Maintainest calmly what thou didst
> 　Before. . . .
>
> Once more for intellectual food
> 　Thou'lt serve: an added phrase or two
> Will make thee really just as good
> 　As new.

And listening crowds that throng the spot,
  True Learning's cup intent to drain,
Will cry, "The old familiar rot
  Again!"

IX

But seriously I tell you to choose your lectures: and to choose a few only; such as will turn you on to lines of reading for yourselves: for over the main course of your studies—

The student who reads has two capital advantages over the student who listens: he can vary the pace at will, and he can turn back and compare passages; and according to my experience as a student, [says Sidgwick] these advantages altogether outweigh the counter-advantage of the additional intelligibility which discourse acquires from the inflections of the human voice and the variations of the speaker's emphasis.

I have hinted to you that he was a charitable man. I myself should have interpolated here the word "sometimes." But, to continue—

For in learning it seems to me fundamentally important to be able to take in rapidly what is easy and familiar, and pause to reflect as long as one likes on what is novel or difficult. No doubt a competent lecturer will always try to vary the length of his treatment and the fulness of his illustrations in various parts of his subject according to his conception of their comparative difficulty. But no lecturer can be sufficiently acquainted with the nature and causes of the transient hesitations and difficulties which beset the intellectual progress of any individual mind; and even if his sympathetic insight were ever so keen and subtle, the diversities in previous knowledge and faculty of apprehension which were commonly found among the members of an actual class render it impossible for him to adapt his exposition closely to the intellectual state of any individual. Besides, the one thing a lecturer cannot allow is a pause for reflection: he must go on talking.

So in this matter of lectures I give you two words of practical advice:

(1) The first that, of the fare our Lecture-list provides for you, you test—not too hastily, but severely after a while—and separate that which you feel to be helping you, discontinuing your attendance at lectures which hold but a vapid interest for you or even invite your attention to wander. It was even in St. Paul an *amende honorable* to restore to life the young Eutychus who fell asleep in a window while he was preaching. But I have known lecturers—and in English too—whose dulness was capable of throwing Eutychus out of a window before they had got ten minutes going.

(2) Secondly, if you have difficulties in your reading, do not wait on lecturers to resolve them. Come to us—to your professors and readers as well as to your supervisors of studies. Tread our stairs. You need not for your self-conceit apply to us Montaigne's words— "If there be any person, any knot of good company, in France or elsewhere who can like my humour, and whose humour I can like, let them but whistle and I will run." But I beg all and any of you, Gentlemen, to believe that our oaks are seldom sported against anyone in search of what counsel we can give. There is a good and ancient phrase up here, "I am reading with so-and-so": and it truly indicates the traditions of the place which we, in our Tripos, would carry on. I beg you to

remember that our justification is bound up in your promise, and that men (say) of my age, or considerably younger, may take much heart from hope in younger men who intrude on our shyness as friends.

X

For another point—You may or may not remember a sentence I quoted a while back from Sidgwick, that "in England, at any rate, it is generally thought that academic teaching, to be effective, must include some kind of exercises written by the student and looked over by the teacher." Well, until lately, no such provision was made in Cambridge for our Tripos, or was made sparsely and sporadically. But I believe that by this time there is scarcely a College which has not provided that an undergraduate reading for the English Tripos shall bring his supervisor some four Essays a term. And the advantage of this is obvious: for not only does it practise the student for examination (on which I would lay the least possible stress): it helps him constantly and periodically to practise the art of literature which he is studying; while it insists on his regularly pausing and clarifying his thought.

Shall I remind you again that we would rather have you able to think accurately and with justice than to acquire any amount of information: that it is no hoard of knowledge we require, but that harder thing, a trained capacity?

XI

For this reason—after a few years' experience—I have come to count these Public Lectures of mine as naught: or as very little in comparison with private and personal talk, or with the very informal classes in which we talk about Aristotle's *Poetics:* concerning which I shall say my final word this morning.

Those of you who take the Tripos on its literary side, as opposed to its philological, will soon see that the two subjects open to them—the special subject of *Tragedy* and the History of *Literary Criticism*—bear intimately upon one another, and that a student who has mastered one has really broken (so to speak) the back of the other.   And the secret of it all is the *Poetics:* in an understanding and, in the mind, a hard skeletonic analysis of that little treatise.   For it matters little if Aristotle was right or Aristotle was wrong—as a number of his interpreters have undoubtedly been wrong.   The point is that without a grounding in this treatise nobody can tell what European Criticism has ever been driving at, or even understand its technology.   It lays its spell on everything and everybody; from Horace to Castelvetro, to Corneille, to Boileau, to Dryden, to Pope, Gray, Johnson, Lessing, Schlegel, Coleridge, Arnold, Sainte-Beuve, Croce—name what names you will.   Unlike the perfect and estimable tractate of Longinus *On the Sublime,* which says everything so well as to close discussion, this wonderful imperfect little work provokes argument at every third sentence.

And precisely because it provokes, and has for centuries provoked, thought—interpreting and misinterpreting, but always eager—and because, too, it dominates even those who dispute it in whole or in part, forcing them to fight on *its* chosen ground and to challenge with *its* intellectual weapons—I would have every reader for our Tripos get its anatomy into his system.   Lacking this, he cannot know what a Ben Jonson or a Brunetière was driving at—and so will miss the mere *history* of the business: but, lacking it, he will more ruinously miss many an opening of free discussion on which—if there be any virtue in the idea of a University—young and alert minds are here to seize.

XII

Some months ago—to be exact on April 23rd, a day of the year famous for greater things—a Committee of men and women who had been sitting at intervals for eighteen months or so collecting evidence, examining witnesses and drawing conclusions on the future of English teaching in England, put their names to an agreed report, the publication of which would seem to be overdue. Indeed in advertising this lecture I promised myself the pleasure of reading some of their conclusions to you. I cannot yet do this without a technical breach of confidence. But I may be allowed to say this—that when the report appears, and you turn to the section on English teaching in our Universities, you will find that in this higher teaching individual experiment is encouraged—that Oxford and Cambridge, London and Liverpool are not required to be of one pattern, and in particular that our Tripos has met its enemies and survived.

Now let me repeat we aim here to train *capacity,* to breed men of a certain intellectual quality rather than to give them, or expect from them, reams of memorised facts and dates. In fact we have sympathy with the artizan who, reproached by a University Extensioner in public lecture for not taking notes, demanded sullenly "And what's my bloomin' head for?" In our efforts we do not spread before you the concurrent feasts of *Paradise Lost* and Pollok's *Course of Time,* the novels

of Hardy or Henry James *and* of Miss Blank: we assume rather that if we get you permeated with the spirit
(say but of the ninth Book) of *Paradise Lost* or of such
a story as *Tess,* you may be safely left to deal with the
Rev. Robert Pollok and with Miss Blank when you
encounter them.

This means that, assuming in you a spirit which
responds to a spiritual appeal—as surely as matter
attracts matter—we seek, after our fashion, to rectify
it, to adjust your judgment, and at the end of the short
while which is at your disposal and ours to send you
forth moderately capable at least of rejecting the evil
or the foolish, and choosing the good, on your own
account and by an acquired instinct.

XIII

But—for my last word today—this requires something more in you than what Wordsworth calls "a wise
passiveness" of sitting and listening. You must learn
to use words; for so only (as Newman demonstrated
in one of the wisest of his discourses) can you learn
to clarify, to define, to express your own thoughts: or
again, as Croce teaches, a thought does not arrive at
being a thought until we rightly express it.

One often hears [says he] people say that they have in their
minds many important thoughts but are unable to express
them. In truth, if they really *had* them they would have
coined them into beautiful ringing words and thus expressed
them.

In other words, you must not believe with Dogberry
that "to write and read comes by nature . . . and for
your writing and reading, let that appear when there is

no need of such vanity." In short you must practise writing. You should write, on subjects connected with your work, at least four essays a term. And in this we your tutors and supervisors can, maybe, help you. We cannot of course supply

> One impulse from a vernal wood,

neither are we sages. Treat us rather as elder brothers —or, if you will and you must, treat us as hard men reaping where we have not sown and gathering where we have not strawed. Only bring us *evidence* of your talents.

ON "THE NEW READING PUBLIC." (I)

That ever-increasing company drawn from what we commonly call the lower-middle class and the working class, who have discovered that the literature of our country is a priceless possession which is their very own, and which they are as eager to read as any normal man would be to explore the highways and byways of a newly acquired estate.

SIDNEY DARK.

I

I WANT to get at the truth about this: and we shall best get at it by first separating our hopes from our experiences.

That "what we call the lower-middle class and the working class" are learning to read in ever-increasing numbers must be gladly admitted—gladly, because the ability to read conditions the whole business, and this ability spreads and widens in our population every day. On this verifiable fact a great deal of hope may reasonably be built—a very great deal of hope as I shall in due course try to show.

But I distrust the assumption—if it be an assumption—that in any encouraging proportion to its vast numbers, this new Reading Public is discovering the literature of our country to be "a priceless possession." Our total population is of course far better educated than the total population of these Islands (say) in 1870, and not only in the mass but on the average. The number of "illiterates"—of persons unable to read either print or handwriting—has shrunk amazingly in the last two generations: and apart from the statistics that confirm this, let any man of sense, knowing England, ask himself if anything like the universal franchise we now enjoy or endure could have been granted to our slow-moving nation by Queen Victoria's advisors in 1870. It may or may not be wise today: in 1870 it would have been incredible.

Moreover the intelligence and adaptability of the average man and woman has increased remarkably in this while. (It is, one might argue, just this improvement which pushed on and on insensibly the further extensions of our franchise.) At any rate if we compare ten years ago with a hundred years ago we may fetch a fairly startling illustration.

Surely this country's share of victory in the late War against Central Europe was won rather by her soldiery than by any genius of her Generals: that is to say— after our immortal "mercenary" force had kept the pass like the Spartans—by a host of civilians educated more or less in the tradition of Forster's much abused Education Act of 1870, who turned to learn warfare quickly in the hour of their Country's necessity, and brought to that job in their degrees the general aptitude to learn they had acquired in their very various schoolings. If our Generals could have relied on no better, no more intelligent material than Wellington had to employ, where should we have been in 1914–1918? "The scum of the earth," were his words for his men; "incapable of any great effort . . . by anything but the fear of immediate corporal punishment." Vilely ungrateful words, of course,

for a soldiery that razed Talavera, carried the hill of
Albuera, stormed Badajoz, died to make him remembered by Salamanca, Vittoria, Waterloo! Still, they
were Wellington's words, and he could use them un-
contradicted. Can anyone conceive of like words being
used by any British Commander in the late War? I
dare to say that, when everything has been said against
the "Industrial Movement"—and in spite of it (as I
hold) through successive efforts at education with local
devotion backing them—our whole Commonwealth had
improved amazingly since Waterloo in intelligence and
morals. If anyone doubt what Education has done for
us, let him study Hogarth, or Rowlandson and Gillray.

Now such an improvement of the general intelligence
must be good for a nation, and for a democracy is indeed
necessary. Mankind has of course pursued the ideal of
democracy through many experiments, and with various
results, mostly disappointing. Strictly speaking, of
course, a democracy is just a form of Government. If
we would take it at its highest valuation, we go, perhaps, to Lincoln's Gettysburg Address, from the Preface
to Wyclif's Bible, and call it "Government of the people,
by the people, for the people." But anyhow in our
present-day State it tends to be Government under
various devices, by *all* the people. That—just and
simply that—everlastingly cheats us in discussing democracy in connection with "culture." We are haunted
by old connotations, old words, which do not apply to
our problem at all.

Athens, for example, was a democracy in the sense
that every citizen had a vote. But the citizens of Athens
were a privileged few in a tiny State; and the privilege
rested on a slave-population denied the franchise. From
Archon down to Sausage-seller its burghers were a

handful of men; a democracy in name, but actually a busy-idle aristocracy, absolved by the luck of the gods from taking its proletariat or its women into account as it made wars and treaties, or again as it discussed pictures or statues or tragedies or mathematics or the relation of man to the Universe. Obviously the difference between that and any modern democracy (unless it be the Republic of Andorra) is immense. In the matter of wars and treaties we of Great Britain do not, to be sure, directly consult the electorate: nevertheless our rulers cannot dare to make wars and treaties unless assured of having the mass of public opinion behind them—this mass expressing itself as a rule through the medium of the Press, another modern invention, unknown to the Athenians. Our obligations as citizens extend not to a squabble with Thebes, but from this small island over an empire the extent of which we are for ever endeavouring to bring home to the imagination of our children, hoping, as we widen that imagination, to increase their sense of responsibility.

On the whole (I think) these efforts to educate the electorate in practical matters have worked fairly well. But although any comparable extension of "culture" must pre-suppose a general improvement of intelligence, I am inclined to doubt if we have yet arrived at making the average citizen a cultivated man in any sense which the average Athenian citizen would have recognised.

And that, in fine, is the doubt which gives me pause. Be it assumed, albeit without complacency, that England is educating her population at reasonable speed in the business of governing itself at home and administering our vast possessions and dependencies abroad, are we at any comparable rate teaching it to acquire those graces of civilization which add happiness to responsibility, or

that understanding of a man's self—of his individual
soul and its place in the scheme of things—which we
recognise as illuminating the best among us, in whose
way of life we surmise a secret that for them makes
obedience and command, duty and liberty, one and the
same thing? There are such men, and of the more
eminent we feel that they should by right be our gov-
ernors. But have we sufficient numbers of men less
eminent to whom we can safely deputise the control
of minor and local affairs in our great and complicated
Commonwealth? Are we breeding such at a rate at all
proportionable with the increase of our population? To
put it in another way—If the British Empire were to
perish tomorrow, or in a hundred years time, as other
majestic empires have perished, doubtless it would be
remembered for its achievement at home of a wonderful
Metropolis set in an area of subservient squalor; of
a Court at once ornate with medieval pageantry, to
impose a sense of exalted superiority, yet sentimentally
beloved as human alike with the rest of us, and the
dearer the oftener it put off its robes and was driven
about in mufti; of a genial, humorous, grumbling and
on the whole contented populace; with many noble build-
ings, schools everywhere, great Universities for the more
fortunate: abroad, for signal achievements in discovering
and colonising distant lands, driving roads, building
bridges, piercing wildernesses with railways, stamping
out slavery, substituting order for chaos, and all by the
courage of men who, grappling with risks and dangers
as occasion arose, had to ignore that any mistake would
be visited upon them by governmental reproof, dismissal,
and the ruin of their careers.

    In face of this you may reasonably ask, What has
"culture" to do with it all? Well, "culture" has become

a suspected word and is almost in danger of becoming an opprobrious one. But, forgetting that for a moment, let us ask by what, if our Empire were to perish to-morrow, it would be remembered after three or four centuries any more *thankfully* than Babylon or Egypt? We have in our Cathedrals many noble and soaring masses of masonry; but their architecture, being Gothic, depends to such an extent upon balance and materials, thrusting, contending, wearing one another out, that even in our day Deans and Chapters constantly cry aloud for money, to prop and underpin: and the death-watch beetle eats the beam, while heavy traffic shakes the foundation.

So with our triumphs of domestic building—the "Stately Homes of England." For good or evil their masters are being ousted by taxation, and their private treasures dispersed among foreign money-lenders. Even a few years will suffice to obliterate their parks and gardens; and a few more—a very few indeed in comparison with the age of the Pyramids or of those Greek and Sicilian Temples which the Turk failed to destroy even by gunpowder—will dilapidate the house.

I choose these, our Cathedrals and our private mansions with their demesnes as monuments, "glories of our blood and state" characteristically English; and yet doomed to decay, as Tintern and Kenilworth have decayed, to pass out into "shadows, not substantial things," as our feudal system has passed out, with its ancient and lordly families. In the words of Lord Chief Justice Crewe, "There must be a period and an end to all temporal things, *finis rerum,* an end of names and dignities and whatsoever is terrene. For where is Bohun? Where is Mowbray? Where is Mortimer? Nay, which is more and most of all, where is Plantagenet? They are intombed in the Urns and Sepulchres of mortality."

Even more certainly than these must the glittering fabric of British Commerce, being more materialistic, dissolve in its hour. Will its hard superseders genuinely grieve

> when even the Shade
> Of that which once was great is passed away?

Will they not determine rather that the end and object of our empire-making and commerce-building was selfish, to enrich ourselves? Who now worships Venice for her former wealth? or who thinks of Corinth, that earlier courtesan town, as he thinks of Athens? Having answered that, let us ask ourselves—Have we English in our record a something to defy time and make successive ages lastingly and consciously thankful for us? Have we in us as a Nation anything akin to that Athenian spirit which compelled Rome, after subduing Athens, to consecrate her as a shrine; which again, after long suppression through the Dark Ages revived from her altar and kindled westward the passion for learning and liberty?

II

Yes, we surely have—in our Literature.

Let me try to remove the suspicion that I assert this in any vocational rapture, or contentiously, as Demetrius the Silversmith extolled Diana or as the shoemaker boasted that there was nothing like leather. I suppose, indeed, at this time of life I may claim to have been in some sort a "man of letters": which, if one keep a due sense of proportion, is a rather jolly thing to be. But in a world which—shaped approximately like a Christmas pudding and containing a million more ingredients —revolves round the Sun under a control in which none of us has a say, it seems foolish to make hierarchies among the honest ways of earning a livelihood.

Still, as a matter of observation and without any naughty pride, one may distinguish these according to their permanent effect on our fellows: and as a matter of human experience Literature—which, simply defined, is memorable speech placed on record—happens to be the most permanent thing known to us, if not in vitality yet always in combining vitality with stability.

It is often forgotten, to be sure—but should not be— that Hellas, in her brief age of flowering, made discoveries in science—in mathematics, in astronomy, in geometry, in physics, even in biology—which all must allow to be as wonderful as her literature, and some may consider even more valuable.

All our sciences, like the names of them, are of Greek origin. Indeed it would be possible to maintain the thesis that this part of our debt to ancient Greece is one of more consequence than all the masterpieces of literature and art she has bequeathed to us. As men possessed of an insatiable love of truth-seeking, a noble madness for seeing things as they are and not as they might be or ought to be, Euclid, Aristotle (as biologist), and Hippocrates (the wise physician) might be rated as more typically Greek than Homer, Sophocles, and Thucydides. The latter have given us undying pictures of men and cities, of human exaltations and agonies which even to-day help us to understand the mysteries of human nature, for even the people of the far-off Homeric Age were more like than unlike ourselves. But the work of the former is indispensable in a higher degree, seeing that it is actually part of the very foundation of the knowledge by, in, and for which the modern world goes on living.[1]

This is true enough. But here comes in a characteristic of Science which we may call at once its virtue and its defect: that it perpetually antiquates itself. Copernicus destroys Ptolemy; Einstein modifies Newton; even in the exact science of mathematics Napier with his logarithms supersedes old methods of calculating; while in such tentative sciences as philology, psychology, economics, new theories and systems obliterate the old ones at such a rate that a very small Library will suffice for the working Student, who may relegate the mass of former "authorities" to a Museum.

On the other hand all great literature—be it poetry, drama, philosophy, history, whatever we will—has the strange inestimable quality of permanence. Homer may tell of gods in whom no one any longer believes. But what does it matter? Religions pass, poetry remains. Plato may be full of mistakes, Dante and Milton may throw their fervour into creeds now discredited, Voltaire employ his industrious wit in mocking them. Shakespeare's theatre may be obsolete. But our daily life is not only the better and saner because these tremendous writers *have been:* it is conditioned always, if we would be cultivated men, by the fact that their works *are.*

---

[1] *Our Debt to Greece and Rome,* by E. B. Osborn (Hodder & Stoughton). I have met with no small book that in a general survey of Greek and Roman culture puts the case for both so lucidly and concisely, as with none better calculated to win the non-classical reader away from any notion that the Classics are "unprofitable." It should be read alongside *The Pageant of Greece,* by R. W. Livingstone, which gives specimen passages of the Greek authors in selected English translations, set among pages of delightful exposition.

It is not my business here to enquire into the mystery, to discover the antiseptic which saves literature from old age; nor need we here attempt to weigh out the claims of our eminent men of science, seamen, statesmen, explorers, colonisers, administrators *et caeterorum* against the claims of our great writers. Indeed such comparisons, if not odious, are usually misleading: and, for an example, Carlyle's question, "Would you sooner, of your possessions, part with Shakespeare or with India?" will never be answered by sensible men, who decline to deal *in impari materia*. It is enough for our purpose that you and I believe our literature to be, in Mr. Dark's phrase, "a priceless possession" and one to deserve, after we are gone, the gratitude of Nations as yet unborn.

But when he tells us that an "ever-increasing company drawn from what we commonly call the lower-middle class and the working class" have discovered this and "are as eager to read as any normal man would be to explore the highways and byways of a newly acquired estate" I think we may pause, not indeed in disbelief— for no one can doubt this company to be increasing— but in the hope that by facing some obstacles we may help the increase by studying to remove them.

III

I suggest then that the first and perhaps the main difficulty found by this new reading public in exploring its newly acquired estate is the simple one that it was neither enclosed nor planted for its new inheritors; that during the earlier centuries of its growth our literature was perforce *aristocratic*.

I say "perforce," and may add "unconsciously":

because this aristocratic quality came to inhere in it through no snobbishness or highbrow pose of conde-scension, but of necessity. It is after all a stipulation of literature (other than the most primitive) that its audience is able to read. The strains of Homer to be sure, as of the old Ballad-singers, were originally trans-mitted and popularised orally by the composers them-selves or by reciters who had committed them to mem-ory: but even the strains of Homer must get put down in writing before an Athenian can—as any Athenian did—handle Homer as his Bible, his Book.

Now if we start, say, with Chaucer, a man bred at Court and acquainted with French, Italian, Latin and possibly some other languages, we are dealing with a man engaged in transferring on paper into English the treasures of these polite languages, in assimilating and in the process transforming them, transfusing them with the spirit of "Merry England," *in a native language which the mass of his fellow-countrymen could not read!*

I desire you, parenthetically, to admire the pluck of these early authors who dared to attempt high poetry in the vernacular and leave great verse unto what was then a little clan; being scholars themselves and there-fore sensible of all the weight of tradition that Latin, the "Universal language" of scholars, alone could be the language of any literature worth scholarly respect. As Newman suggests—When we consider such innovators as Dante and Chaucer, we must marvel not only at the genius of what they did but that they had the genius to do it at all.

Nevertheless an artist can only work with tools, upon material; with the intention too (unless he be a very hermit) of pleasing somebody besides himself, be that somebody one or many. For example, if Lorenzo the

Magnificent command a piece of plate, the artist employs his best skill upon gold or silver to gratify Lorenzo; or if a statue to adorn a city, then upon a statue to gratify Lorenzo and his citizens as well; or if a play, then one to gratify Lorenzo and the audience, which again may be a select audience of courtiers or a popular one of all sorts and conditions. Now the men who may be called the creators of our literature worked with tools they had largely to invent, and worked under the fascination of the Classics whom they strove to emulate, amid a population mostly illiterate. They were educated men addressing an educated few, their prose and poetry alike φωνᾶντα συνετοῖσι.

Also, the dramatists apart, they did not write for gain; and the dramatists themselves could hope for little gain from print. Either they published, as Ben Jonson did, in hope of immortality, or were content, as Shakespeare was (and we know Shakespeare to have been a shrewd man of business), to leave any masterpiece to its fate, to the moth and spider in dusty theatrical cupboards. In days when the diligent copyist of an old MS. could command far higher pay than an original writer, authors in general had to rely for anything beyond fame on the gifts of princes or the largesse of noble patrons. Some few, who could afford it of their private means, might publish for their own or their friends' delectation, or, like Sir Thomas Browne, to defend their reputation, their manuscripts having been handed around and vulgarised in copies full of mistakes. In this way for example (as he tells us in his preface) Browne's *Religio Medici* attained print, while his *Christian Morals* first saw the light some thirty-odd years after his death, its editor, the Venerable John Jeffery, D.D., Archdeacon of Norwich, explaining—

The reason why it was not Printed sooner is because it was unhappily Lost, by being Mislay'd among other MSS. for which Search was lately made in the Presence of the Lord Archbishop of Canterbury.

Generations of aspiring authors had to trim their sails between servile dependence and Grub Street penury before Fielding could hint, in his preface to *Tom Jones*, at a port of popular recompense ahead—

An author ought to consider himself, not as a gentleman who gives a private or eleemosynary treat, but rather as one who keeps a public Ordinary, at which all persons are welcome for their money.

Even today any practise of poetry—our greatest National art—must be taken with the slenderest hope of reward. We love it and let it starve: which means that we drive it into little coteries of people who live in hot-houses upon mutual adulation; again a sort of aristocracy in its way, but tenuous, unaërated, uncivil—as a Greek would say "idiotic"—because forced back upon its own private standards of value. Such an attitude towards any form of art seems to me, Gentlemen, morose and out of place in our Commonwealth. It inclines the patient, for example, to say of any exotic statue offensive to the public, "Stand aside, or pass it with acceptance, until you have learnt that it is good for you. *We* are the *cognoscenti* and proclaim it to be good without giving reasons which you would not understand." Now really this will not do for a well-ordered State. The appeal of the greatest art is always far simpler, more understandable, than this attitude presupposes. The Athenians insisted on beautiful, intelligible form in their public statues, that their pregnant women, passing these, might insensibly mould to birth beautiful children.

IV

In calling, then, the bulk of our great literature "aristocratic," I do not mean that it is consciously esoteric or highbrow or patronizing, condescending. Indeed, as Emerson has pointed out, and as I shall insist by and by, the great authors never condescend. I simply mean that historically, by force of geniture and circumstance (at any rate until the last century was well advanced), it had to address a few before conciliating the many.

I do not forget that many early translations were made by these scholars with the express aim of popularising the Scriptures and the Classics : nor will I slur over such eminently popular writers as Bunyan, Defoe, Dickens. But their number would have to be greatly multiplied to oppose my argument. For these men were exceptions, striking exceptions that prove the rule, as you may convince yourselves by glancing over the field in rapid survey. We may start with Chaucer, a page at Court, pensioned later to give him leisure for poetry; or with moral Gower, a man of estate, whose effigy rests in Southwark Cathedral, his head pillowed upon three prodigious tomes of his own composition—one in Latin, another in French, the third in English and comprising thirty thousand lines of polite verse. The imitators or immediate descendants of these two are courtly or academic poets, so dull that they almost quench the flame. But it leaps to life again—in whom? In Sir Thomas Wyat and the Earl of Surrey, courtiers both, translators of French and Italian courtliness; in Sir Thomas More and other inheritors of the proud

Renaissance spirit; in Spenser, discussing with Gabriel
Harvey whether to write *The Faerie Queene* in English
rhyme or in classical hexameters.   It passes on through
the dramatists, the "University wits" and their play-
house rivals—Marlowe mad with Renaissance *virtu* and
classical inspiration, Kyd steeped in Seneca, Ben Jonson
pedantically Latin and Plautine.   Nay, with Shakespeare
himself (of disputed education) you may take up *Venus
and Adonis* and judge if he be not classical by intent; or
count the heroes and heroines in his *dramatis personae,*
reckoning the proportion of kings, queens, princes, lords
and ladies in any chance play, and then deny, if you can,
that he followed dramatic tradition in preferring the
great of this earth whether for comedy, history or
tragedy.   Or again you may find much pretty practice
in separating the gift of high poetical speech with which
he endows his lordlier creatures from the cheap and
often dirty chat he assigns to his low comedians.   I
need not stress the continuance of this aristocratic
tradition right down through Bacon, Donne, Milton,
Dryden, Pope, Congreve. . . .   What sort of general
public did Sir Thomas Browne address?—or Addison,
or Dr. Johnson, or Berkeley, or Burke, or Gibbon?—or,
to come later, Landor, or Matthew Arnold, or Walter
Pater—or even Coleridge, preaching critical faith with
Biographia Literaria for title; or Ruskin, printing mis-
sionary discourses under such labels as *Fors Clavigera,
Aratra Pentelici?*

Let us go back to Milton for a minute.   Milton wished
well to the popular cause, as he conceived it, and wrote
in the interests of a "democratic" form of religion.   But
who can turn the pages of *Paradise Lost* or *Samson
Agonistes* and doubt that he was addressing a close
audience of scholars?   I open a page and read:

His legions, angel forms, who lay entranced,
Thick as autumnal leaves that strew the brooks
In Vallombrosa, where the Etrurian shades
High over-arch'd embower; or scattered sedge
Afloat, where with fierce winds Orion armed
Hath vext the Red Sea coast, whose waves o'erthrow
Busiris and his Memphian chivalry.

To suppose that Milton intended the above passage for any wide reading public is plainly absurd. Nor can one even begin to understand the geography of Heaven, Paradise, Eden, Chaos, Hell in that most mathematically arranged poem without some knowledge of the Ptolemaic and Copernican systems together and in opposition. Nay, one has often to read Ptolemy or Galen into Shakespeare when Shakespeare talks of the stars or of human disorders.[1] On top of such obstacles against admitting "the lower-middle and working classes" to their priceless possession, we are tending more and more to exclude Latin and Greek from our educational system on the ground that the study of them does not pay! Well, for that matter it surely must be common ground with us all that no form of art, or of literature, no civic virtue, no daily courtesies, no domestic love, ever "paid." These count among the things above pay, being above price.

Thus far, Gentlemen, we have dealt among difficulties and dwelt on them. Next time I hope to be more constructive, possibly more helpful.

[1] For an instance, pointed out the other day by my friend Dr. Dover Wilson, when Falstaff exclaims "A plague of sighing and grief! It blows a man up like a bladder," we miss half the point of the jest unless we know that Falstaff, contemplating his stomach, is topsy-turvying the fashionable medical doctrine that sighing and grief emaciate the body. An Elizabethan audience would have jumped to it in a flash.

ON "THE NEW READING
PUBLIC" (II)

I

I ONCE gave a course of Lecures on *The Art of Reading;* and shall take leave today to select some sentences from these as axioms which may serve us in discussing our particular problem of The New Reading Public.

Axiom 1. The master-key to literature, as indeed to almost all rooms of knowledge, is Silent Reading.

At first sight this looks like a truism: since acquaintance with literature must naturally presuppose some ability to read. But in this Country of ours the prefixing of an audible "h" to a vowel, and its omission, may sometimes carry different meanings, implications, even consequences; and if for ability we substitute the good old word "hability"—"hability to read"—we get a shade of meaning which carries a very considerable difference indeed: since merely to be "able to read" or "have the ability to read" may in common speech convey no more than that you can, if you try, make sounds corresponding to a written sentence: whereas "hability" connotes power acquired by practice, with corresponding ease; so that you can fix your attention on the author's meaning, or have leisure to judge his style or his method, relieved of any difficulty in construing his language; unless it be obscure, when your judgment tells you whether (as with Shakespeare or other great authors) his obscurity be worth your intelligent application or (as with most authors who write obscurely) it come of his own incompetence. Of this, again, increasing "hability" will in time make you a pretty fair judge. Also it will save much labour by training you to "skip" judiciously—a sound accomplishment, believe me, and used by the best critics. I remember a saying of the late Henry Jackson's, dropped in some casual talk about scholarship, that the mastery of a difficult tongue, though the reward of hard work, usually came all of a sudden. "I can't recall how long I worked at Greek before one day, in the midst of a Chorus of Sophocles, I discovered that I was construing it readily and realized that I had come to know the language, to move about in it."

But any such "hability" even in our mother tongue must presume an elementary ability to read: and so we make a start, as I fear everybody must—or at any rate everybody does—upon the Child. I am very sorry for it, my sympathies being all with "the small apple-eating urchin whom we know," as Bagehot calls him. But there it is. In the old mythologies, you remember, Atlas supported the world, and the firmament on top of it, upon his shoulders; and Atlas stood on a tortoise; and the tortoise stood on—I forget what at this moment, but think it must have been on the head of a Child. Yes, since the end of the War (which by the way he did not make) we are all agreed upon starting the reconstruction of society with the Child, and *we* are going to tell him how to do it.

Left to himself, he might begin to do it in his own way. Here indeed I must tell one of the truest parables I know of the War. An English regiment in 1918 was marching back in triumph through one of the redeemed towns of Flanders; and our soldiers, carrying each a stick of chocolate in his haversack, scattered the sweets among the cheering children; and the children scrambled for them. But the younger ones, having never tasted or seen chocolate, and mistaking the slabs for toy bricks, carried them off and began to play solemnly at building houses with them. That was *their* idea of reconstruction.

Yes, again, I think Atlas's tortoise—the same perhaps that cracked the skull of Aeschylus (see the Mythologies)—must test its weight on the brain of a Child; whose small bruised heel may rest, maybe, upon the neck of a serpent coiled upon a mill-stone on the floor and ooze of the sea. And so, although I believe "humanism" in reading to be so simple a thing that it lies within the reach of the elderly ("A grandfather can play at it"), I am going to follow the fashion and begin with the Elementary School. But I do not pretend that I am necessarily following the order of nature, as Aristotle would say, and beginning at the beginning. Nor does it matter because there is really neither beginning nor end to this round game. I start with a class in such a School because one must break the circle at some point, and it seems most useful to take the Child as "father of the man" in the sense that Wordsworth intended.

Well, the trouble in an Elementary School is the lack of opportunity for silent reading.

I speak from some experience, having served for more than twenty years on a Local Education Authority and in that time visited a large number of Elementary Schools, some of them many times over. Well-meaning persons are constantly urging us to crowd the syllabus with new subjects, especially "Vocational" subjects. I assert of experience and observation that such subjects, desirable as they seem in themselves, should weigh almost as nothing against the paramount duty of keeping the syallabus clear—in the upper standards most certainly—for one hour's silent reading every day. For this is the ultimate key; the master-key to all literature, to all science. Give the child *that:* then all the rest depends on his own ability, industry, courage.

For, be it remembered, these children have no room, no opportunity, no light as a rule, no table-space, for "evening preparation," "home lessons." Their father returns tired from his day's work and with pardonable gruffness orders them to "Get out and play." There is often but one lamp, kept on the move from kitchen to scullery and back; there is no library. (I am speaking generally of course, but you know this to be true of hundreds of thousands of children. At this point I call up the remembered vision of an urchin curled in the dusk on a door step in a narrow street and tracing out a map of Palestine, his feet tucked out of the way of traffic. That is how *he* was building Jerusalem in England's green and pleasant land.)

I am extremely chary of giving advice to teachers, who usually know their own business a great deal better than the multitude of their counsellors—in whom, with all respect to Solomon, I know that there is not always wisdom. Still I always suspect, as I get to the door of a School house and hear a teacher's voice uplifted within on a high monotonous strain of talk, that I am on the threshold of an unsatisfactory School. The perfect School-hour is one in which the children are quiet and the teacher himself almost as quiet, just occupied in going around and explaining difficulties.

I scarcely need to add that this silent reading must be acquired *through* reading aloud, or that reading aloud should be continued, at short intervals, to the end. This not only helps to correct faulty pronunciation—a point on which I lay no particular stress, because good pronunciation should not be confined to any particular lesson but taught all the time, and best when insensibly, by the teacher's example. The chief value of audible reading resides in its wedding the ear to the voice, and so, gradually, the mind's ear to the written words; until the Child, who naturally loves rhythm and practises it in his games, finds out for himself that written poetry and written prose have their own right rhythms, some simple, others curious, and adapts himself to them. Such a process in my experience out-values all the books on English Prosody ever written (and, by the way, walks quietly past the infection most incident to Prosodians, which is bad temper). By it, through simple practice, the cultivated ear will scan with ease almost any line of almost any poet ordinarily reputed difficult—a line of Donne's for example; will scan it, that is, as Donne scanned it.

But I am pressing too far ahead with this business of silent reading, which after all belongs to the mechanics of the thing. It is time to turn back and consider the *spiritual* side of a Child's guidance into literature.

II

We come then to

Axiom 2. All spirit is mutually attractive, as all matter is mutually attractive.

That is an ultimate fact, and we cannot go beyond it. "Spirit to spirit"—as in water face answereth to face, so the heart of man to man.

It is also the great and central axiom: and I call it so

boldly, because it is not mine. The above sentence, so simple and (you may say) so commonplace, leapt out on me from the page of a little book by a great American scholar, and has long been my soul's comfort. It consists of just eleven words: and we have in them a law of spiritual gravitation; a principle only to be modified by the principle of "relativity" which shall be laid down in our next Axiom. For the moment I wish you to understand the depth of its simplicity. It means that in each one of us there exists a spark, tiny in comparison with the illuminating fire of great genius, but congenitally capable of answering to it as like to like or rather as the same to the same; nay, even filially, emotionally, answering to it as the creature yearns towards its creator with an "Abba, Father!" But I have preached on this text so often and insistently that I shall content myself here with a simple illustration of the instinct, followed by some necessary warnings.

Most healthy children take instinctively to a fairy tale, especially with a Prince and a Princess in it. They have imagination enough to like splendid things and to "feel that they are greater than they know." Even the clutch of a newly-born infant around the nurse's finger has a mysterious tenacity and strength in comparison with its other helplessness.

Again, most healthy children, long before making acquaintance with the real ardours and tremors of love, are in love with it already by anticipation; eager to assist Cinderella into the slipper, to see the enchanted Prince win through the dark forest, to help in foiling the Wizard's spells and uniting true hearts to live happy ever after.

That being so, almost every Child will love the *story* of *The Tempest,* just because it is a tale of this sort, opening too with a magnificent storm, ship-wreck, terror and expectation, all to be cleared away over the shore of an enchanted Island. And he will love it the more through his natural instinct for rhythm and harmony; and yet the more if he be lucky in the guidance of an elder who has made landfall of that Island in his time and by melodious reading can help the voice of Ariel, the vision of those yellow sands.

Something like that is what I mean by saying that "humanism" in Literature can start to be inculcated with the Child's first reading lesson at School. If I add my conviction that this interest will grow in delight with its growth in all sorts of knowledge—acquaintance with actual life, with language, history, Shakespeare's other poetry and the poetry of other writers—you will perhaps agree with me that instinct has started the Child upon his true imaginative development. He has begun upon that which Shakespeare *meant*.

In all but exceptional Children, however, this instinct must be guided tenderly. Longfellow, for example, was no great poet, though a better one than many clever people realize. Anyhow he was a poet, and his poetry directly attracts children by its movement, its colour, its sense of adventure and the "long thoughts" that boyhood nurses:

> I remember the black wharves and the slips,
>   And the sea-tides tossing free;
> And Spanish sailors with bearded lips,
> And the beauty and mystery of the ships,
>   And the magic of the sea.

with

> Sails of silk and ropes of sendal

or the building and launching of "The Ship"

Then the Master,
With a gesture of command,
Waves his hand;
And at the word,
Loud and sudden there was heard,
All around them and below,
The sound of hammers, blow on blow,
Knocking away the shores and spurs.
And see! she stirs!
She starts—she moves—she seems to feel
The thrill of life along her keel,
And, spurning with her foot the ground,
With one exulting, joyous bound,
She leaps into the ocean's arms!
And lo! from the assembled crowd
There rose a shout, prolonged and loud,
That to the ocean seemed to say,—
"Take her, O bridegroom, old and grey,
Take her to thy protecting arms,
With all her youth and all her charms!"

Further, his sentiment, if commonplace, is always clean and untouched by that subtle vulgarity which infects so much of his far more brilliant and far more poetical compatriot Edgar Allan Poe. In short Longfellow is good company for a Child, though the Child should develop no further; yet so modest withal that he insensibly promises a better land ahead, as a kindly Uncle might tell a tale on the *Odyssey* and wind up with "Ah, one of these days you shall read Homer for yourself, my boy!"

Or we may take Macaulay's *Lays*. Matthew Arnold was utterly wrong in suggesting that these encourage bad taste, or that a liking for them supposes bad taste. So far as they go the *Lays* are sound, sane, clean as a whistle; and it is a poor game, anyhow, to discourage a boy's thrill over Horatius at the bridgehead and teach him to feel like a little prig at a moment when even the ranks of Tuscany could scarce forbear to cheer.

> Nought spake he to Lars Porsena,
> To Sextus nought spake he. . . .
> But he saw on Palatinus
> The white porch of his home. . . .

For that passage has more than one of the high attributes of Poetry. It universalises; and it universalises a grand virtue, patriotism: and again, by universalising, its spirit kindles spirit and makes the patriotism disinterested.

For another example of this.—I remember the late Lord Courtney of Penwith once reciting Browning's *Hervé Riel* to an audience of sea-faring men. It is, as you know, the story of how a simple Breton pilot saved his country's fleet from the pursuing English. The audience forgot to remember who was French and who English. They were just sailormen and they held their breath over the following, to release it and cheer like mad at the end—

Still the north-wind, by God's grace!
See the noble fellow's face
As the big ship, with a bound,
Clears the entry like a hound,   [profound!
Keeps the passage as its inch of way were the wide sea's
    See, safe thro' shoal and rock,
    How they follow in a flock,
Not a ship that misbehaves, not a keel that grates the ground,
    Not a spar that comes to grief!
The peril, see, is past,
All are harboured to the last,
And just as Hervé Riel hollas "Anchor"!—sure as fate
Up the English come, too late!

And this sends me up to Shakespeare for another simple story to illustrate my point.   Some years ago I helped in collecting a theatreful of children to witness a performance of *Much Ado about Nothing* by a Benson company in which Mr. and Mrs. Matheson Lang played Benedick and Beatrice.   The children came from scattered districts in a rural county, and I doubt if half a dozen of them had ever sat in a Theatre before.   On the return journey, at a Junction where they had to be shepherded into trains, one small girl stood on the platform as in a trance repeating, "Only to think that any man could ever be so splendid as that Benedick—so splendid—so splendid!"

That was the impression produced by Shakespeare, well acted, upon an almost untutored mind.   Will any of you doubt that it was a wholly beneficent one, enlarging her gaze and making her better by the revelation? Yet, a few "social reconstructors" doubted the wisdom of our taking children to see Shakespeare played in a theatre.

God help the childish, and forgive the wise!

III

This brings us to our next Axiom.

Axiom 3.   All critical discernment, or taste, is relative, notwithstanding that the instinct for it, if it can be found, is absolute.

It is the more important that we lay firm hold on this very simple Axiom because it happens to be the one that our most admired critics of today, from men of European reputation down to our weekly instructors in the *Intelligentsia* Press, persistently miss or, in their impatience, ignore.   They have yielded to the doctrine of

the last two generations that criticism should be a record
of individual impressions produced by any work of art,
and have cunningly wedded this doctrine in practice to
the old judicial or pontifical attitude of the Quarterly
Reviewers under whom Keats and Shelley and Hazlitt
suffered—and this without the old excuse of applying
well-understood "Rules," which could be challenged
either as rules or in their application.

No doubt there is something to be said for this

> Simple plan
> That they should praise who have the power
> And they should curse who can

for our present-day critics are (I think) a more competent lot than those of a generation ago; possibly because
a considerable number of them are themselves engaged
in creative work and therefore able to judge artistry
"from the inside." The body of our writers in this year
of Grace cannot fairly be likened, as Goldsmith likened
their predecessors in his day, to a Persian army, composed of a few fighting men with an innumerable host
of cooks, sutlers, women and camp-followers. But our
stout soldiery might take warning from the fate of the
Praetorian Guard—which, moreover, started as a well-
regimented corps.

My private quarrel is not with their competence, but
with their arrogance. I happen to be a Professor, and
Professors are their favourite butt, possibly because they
are the silentest. Yet I have never met in actual life
with a Professor to match our scorners in the ease with
which they picnic in Sion!

My real grievance, however, is purely impersonal, and
may be divided into two. In the first place the present-

day critic seems unable to realise that while he has been
improving upon his predecessors, the great middle-class
he so constantly derides has been improving itself concurrently, and even to the degree of reading and ad-
miring his own admirable work.

Let me choose an illustration from the illustrious.
Among the acutest of these I account Mr. Arnold
Bennett, who either does not repent of those articles in
which for our pre-War amusement he used to scarify
this middle-class, or "backbone," for its taste, or must
confess that things are (thanks partly to him) better
than they were. Listen to what he was saying some
twenty years ago:

> But it is well for novelists to remember that, in the present
> phase of society and mechanical conditions of the literary
> market, their professional existence depends on the fact that
> the dullest class in England takes to novels merely as a
> refuge from its own dullness. And while it is certain that
> no novelist of real value really pleases that class, it is equally
> certain that without its support (willing or unwilling—
> usually the latter) no novelist could live by his pen. Remove
> the superior stolid comfortable, and the circulating libraries
> would expire. And exactly when the circulating libraries
> breathed their last sigh the publishers of fiction would
> sympathetically give up the ghost. If you happen to be a
> literary artist, it makes you think—the reflection that when
> you dine you eat the bread unwillingly furnished by the
> enemies of art and progress!

Well, he cannot, even in excessive modesty, talk like
that now-a-days. A true artist, he has educated this
class to read his books with avidity and to enjoy them,
which is a good step towards appreciating them.

And this brings me to my second complaint. The

present-day critic apparently cannot see that it takes all
sorts to make a world, and that the world would be a
deadly dull place if we all had his accomplishment. Even
the citizens of Athens—that handy little State—were by
no means impeccable critics: they, and the Judges they
elected, went wrong again and again over their awards
in the public contests of their tragic and comic dramatists.
Also life would be dull for any one of us who started
upon our reading or writing with a taste already refined:
for refinement in literary judgment is one of the few
consolations of old age.

Yes, and considering the fallibility of all human judgment, the extravagances of fashion, the high probability
that our idols of today will be stoned by our children
and pass, if to immortality, through mockery by the
clever and neglect by the dull; considering that, after all,
it takes *some* standard of mental attainment to read a
good poem or a good novel with partial understanding;
considering also that today's literature has its today's
use in helping men and women on their transitory way;
I take no shame in sympathising with this New Reading
Public. I can sympathise with the Rural Library movement as it is being developed by our County Councils.
I can even sympathise with the tired village wife who
sends her child out to borrow from the travelling van a
"Something, my dear, with a love-story in it, that ends
happily."

IV

Axiom 4. *No book can mean the same to any two
men.*

For as no two men leave identical finger-prints, or
have identical convolutions in their brains, so no two men
carry away precisely the same impression from a land-

scape, or a public spectacle or a theatrical performance, or a book.

We may add of course that no two men have precisely the same philosophy or the same religion.   Philosophers may refine as they will, or sacerdotalists try to pack what should be the common belief of a million votaries into a *credo*.   But they merely push the difficulty a stage further, since neither definition nor creed can fix a complete unanimity of understanding—which understanding again may be intellectual and emotional, or ignorant, in infinitely various proportion.

There are thousands of magnificent landscapes in the world, all from moment to moment shifting their colour and visibility with the sun's altitude or the passing of clouds, no two clouds alike; and each at every moment reflecting itself differently on the retina of each separate beholder, whose optic nerve conveys it to an individual brain, and this again with varying import according as the beholder sees it for the first, for the second, up to the nth time, bringing endlessly divers capacities for surprise or aesthetic judgment, endlessly divers associations of ideas, memories, emotions evoked by memory. The first sight of Himalaya for instance, or of the Bay of Naples, which overpowers A may not move in any like degree the equally sensitive $B,$ or not so profoundly as will some trivial rural spot revisited and remembered—

> Four ducks on a pond,
> A grass bank beyond,
> A blue sky of spring,
> White clouds on the wing:
> What a little thing
> To remember for years—
> To remember with tears!

So it is with books: and so even with sentences in books,
lines of poetry, even single words. Take the word
"Home" for example. The French have it not: and
to every one of us it means something different and in
different collocations—

> But he saw on Palatinus
> The white porch of his home. . . .

"Home thoughts from abroad," "Home, deary
home!" "Jerusalem, my happy home"—

> My blood so red
>   For thee was shed,
> Come home again, come home again;
> My own sweet heart, come home again!

> When the voices of children are heard on the green,
>   And whisperings are in the dale, . . .
> Then come home, my children, the sun is gone down. . . .

> Perhaps the self-same song that found a path
>   Through the sad heart of Ruth, when, sick for home,
>   She stood in tears amid the alien corn; . . .

You see that, though not quite as the song means it,
there is no place *like* Home: it is a fixed place in one
sense, and yet it is everywhere.

It follows from this Axiom of ours that there can be
no such thing as "The Hundred Best Books." To be
sure, there are certain books we all ought to read if we
would have any sense of literature in perspective. We
ought to read some Chaucer at least, with some of
Wyat, Surrey, Spenser, Marlowe, Ben Jonson, Donne;
almost all of Shakespeare; some Milton, to try the
young tooth upon; Walton's *Lives, The Pilgrim's Pro-*

gress; some Dryden, including the *Essay of Dramatic Poesy;* and so on, and so on. That is the sort of first list I prescribe for any intelligent young man, telling him further to possess himself of some conspectus of English Literature (Saintsbury's *Short History* for choice) that he may get the greater and lesser writers—or those generally accounted greater or lesser—into his mental perspective. If he have no acquaintance with Greek or Latin, Italian or Spanish or French, I further adjure him to read some Homer, Plato, Virgil, Dante, Don Quixote, Molière in translations, all to help his understanding of our own literature.

But even if we could, in a conclave of critics in a Jerusalem Chamber, conjure up such a phantasm as "The Hundred Best Books," our list would infallibly include several that were of little or no service for some of us, while omitting (and this is more important) several that to some of us would be priceless. And, moreover, as Bacon says, "Some Books are to be tasted, others to be swallowed, and some few to be chewed and digested; That is, some Books are to be read only in parts; others to be read but not curiously, and some few to be read wholly, and with diligence and attention." In general my counsel would be—Read such books as attract you; with such books as, although you find them repellant, help you towards an end that attracts you, using them for mastery of the means to that end.

V

This leads me to conclude with two pragmatic Axioms:
Axiom 5. Libraries are armouries, not gymnasia: and no provision of them will ever exempt us from the civic duty of training minds to use them.

A Public Library is a very good thing: but we must not be misled by easy publicists who call it "a poor man's University." It no more resembles a University than a Railway Book-stall resembles a real Library. A University is a place (*a*) where a number of trained Scholars and men of Science pursue by research, experiment, the higher branches of learning for learning's own sake: (*b*) where a number of young men congregate to be trained in the methods of this learning: (*c*) where these young men, thus congregating from far homes, and thus for three or four years centralised, exchange ideas, discuss problems of life, all with the ardour of youth; in the process sloughing off rusticity, acquainting themselves with many opinions, in rivalry preparing themselves for the race of life while insensibly acquiring that knowledge of the world which in practice can hardly be separated from Charity itself. The Office of the Public Library is humble; and the true business of the Library Committee consists in providing books copiously but judiciously, yet not assuming of their own prejudice that one kind of book is better than another. The function of the good Librarian resembles that of the good Professor: he stands by, and of his knowledge guides the applicant who seeks the better or the best.

Axiom 6. The purpose of Lectures is to awaken and stimulate interest. As vehicles of information they have been almost entirely superseded by books.

I have lectured on Lectures elsewhere. The most of them are, as the late Henry Sidgwick said, "an antiquated survival; a relic of the times before the printing-press was invented." For, when all has been granted to the possibility of inspiration in the spoken word, he who reads has two capital advantages over the auditor in a Lecture-room. He can (1) vary the pace at will, and

(2) he can turn back and compare passages, or work his way back again over some difficult ones; whereas the spoken Lecturer does not consider his particular difficulties, but proceeds within his allotted hour at a nearly equal pace from beginning to end, over rough or smooth.

VI

I hope, Gentlemen, that the Axioms I have laid down for you this morning may be of some help to you, or at any rate that they contain some hope for you who have to face this problem of the New Reading Public. They are at any rate disinterested, since this public will never have any use for me in my time. But I have always believed in books and in my fellow-men alike: and so will conclude by commending to you these grave words from the *Philobiblon* of Richard de Bury, who flourished between the thirteenth and fourteenth centuries:

O Celestial gift of divine liberality, descending from the Father of light to raise up the rational soul even to heaven. . . . Undoubtedly, indeed, thou hast placed thy desirable tabernacle in books, where the Most High, the Light of light, the Book of Life, hath established thee. Here then all who ask receive, all who seek find thee, to those who knock thou openest quickly. In books cherubim expand their wings, that the soul of the student may ascend and look around from pole to pole, from the rising and the setting sun, from the north and from the sea. In them the most high and incomprehensible God Himself is contained and worshipped.

W. S. GILBERT

I

I HAD parted, at the Cambridge Post Office, with a young friend of parts who "deplores" (as he puts it) our whole heritage of English poetry and holds with reason that it ought to make a fresh start. Musing on this assurance of his, on my way to the Botanic Garden, and resigning myself, as my custom is, to grieving

> when even the Shade
> Of that which once was great is passed away,

I encountered two long lines of men on opposite sides of the thoroughfare; the one drawing, or seeking to draw, Unemployment Pay; the other taking, or seeking to take, tickets for Gilbert-and-Sullivan Opera.

"Ah, there," thought I, "after all, the last enchantment of the Victorian age has captured you, my lads, and holds you by the Achilles tendon!" For I recognise your faces. You are the same that, the other day, were affecting to despise

> Come down, O maid, from yonder mountain height—

or

> O lyric love, half angel and half bird!

But as soon as it comes to "Tit-willow!" or "The Policeman's lot is not a happy one," you are held and "laid by the heel."

Now I wish to enquire into this and the reason of it; and, believe me, not sardonically. My first introduction to Gilbert-and-Sullivan Opera dates back just fifty years, to an amateur performance of *H.M.S. Pinafore* that enchanted a child. The first play I ever saw in a London theatre was *Patience,* in the course of its first run at the Opéra Comique. As an undergraduate I have taken as much trouble as any of you to listen to *The Sorcerer, Princess Ida, The Mikado;* and my own two favourites, *Iolanthe* and *The Gondoliers,* still conjure up by association all manner of happy memories. I yet can surrender myself (at intervals) to Gilbert-and-Sullivan with an abandon you may ascribe to the natural gaiety of declining years, or to sentimentality—which you will. Let that pass: for, with your leave, the question affects not *me* but *you.* Why do you who expend so much cleverness in deriding the more serious contemporaries of W. S. Gilbert and Arthur Sullivan, yet experimentally confess to this one most typically late-Victorian enthusiasm which binds your spiritual contemporaries with your fathers and grandfathers?

You at any rate will not plead—you, who follow so eagerly all the many experiments of our Festival Theatre in substituting mechanics for drama—that you cling to a tradition of the provinces. That provincial audiences flock to these Operas even as you do; that amateurs throughout England spend their winters in rehearsing one and another of them; that regularly, in the week following Easter, the railways convey down baskets of regulation wigs and costumes from Covent Garden to remote towns and Village Institutes—all this is certain.

And I doubt not that the executors and holders of the Gilbert-and-Sullivan copyrights have worked out commercial reasons for feeding the provinces with these Operas while denying them to the Metropolis. But as little do I doubt that, for some while to come, a noble presentation of the whole cycle in London would draw packed houses. This abstention is a mystery to me, but it does not affect the argument; the first point of which is that all over England, after forty-odd years, generations of young and intelligent people keep renewing their delight in Gilbert-and-Sullivan Opera.

II

Now this, when we consider how typically late-Victorian these Operas are—how limited in range of idea, even of invention—how much of their quiddity (in *Patience,* for example) belongs to its hour in a past era; may well give us a shock. It might also give me occasion to ask, why some of you, and those not the least intelligent, haunt these Operas, although in clever debate you think it not unseemly to deride Meredith for a mountebank and Tennyson for a maiden aunt?

But I seem to know you too well to believe that in your heart of hearts you cherish any such foolish opinions, at any rate ineradicably, or truly believe Gilbert and Sullivan to be the lone Dioscuri of our late-Victorian night. Let us start on the plain common ground that, after forty years or so, their work continues to delight young and old, and try to account for it.

III

The appeal of Music being, by virtue of its indefiniteness, so much more elusive of date than the spoken or written word, and especially if the subject be at all "topical," shall we hold that Gilbert survives mainly through Sullivan's music? Vaguely we may feel Sullivan's melody to be as Victorian as are Gilbert's plots and tricks and whole theatrical concept; but these, having to be framed in words and on lines of logic—and topsy-turvy logic is yet logic and the basis of Gilbert's wit—can be brought to tests which music airily eludes. They are written in words and can be attacked in words; and must continue to suffer this comparative disadvantage until critics of music find a method of expressing their likes and dislikes by musical notation.

But no; this explanation will not serve. For Gilbert, very much of his period and exposed to all the perils which must beset any man who would attract a theatrical audience by wit and song, was yet (if you will search his *libretti*) extremely wary of topical allusions that might date him. In *Patience,* to be sure (one of his earliest), he shot at, and winged, a passing mode. But excepting a passing allusion to the late Captain Shaw of London's Fire Brigade and a somewhat pointed one in *Utopia, Limited* to the light refreshment provided for *débutantes* at Queen Victoria's Drawing-Rooms, you will seek his work in vain for topical references. To be sure, in *H.M.S. Pinafore* (his earliest success) he poked obvious fun at Mr. W. H. Smith, First Lord of the Admiralty: but there exists a most illuminating letter of his in which he hopes he has removed all suspicion of personal offence by indicating that the victim was a Liberal!—a letter which should be a *locus classicus* for research into the ultimate obtuseness of wit. Dealing with his times as he knew them, he could not of course foresee that events would in time blunt the application of one of his neatest shafts—the Sentry's song in *Iolanthe.* But I think we may agree that in this slow-moving country of ours Gilbert's raillery has worn as well as the absurd institutions against which he not too seriously aimed at. They are accustomed to that sort of thing, and have allowed him to wear just as well as they have worn.

I suggest that if you mark and note this avoidance of topical allusion in Gilbert, you will come to the conclusion with me that the man considered himself as one writing for posterity, as carefully at least as Horace Walpole did in composing his familiar letters to Horace Mann. But on this point I shall presently have more evidence to bring. For the moment let his forty-odd years' success stand for presumptive evidence that— Sullivan apart—Gilbert wrote with intent to last.

This intention apart, it were unjust to hold that Gilbert lives by the grace of Sullivan. Offenbach's music was as tunable as Sullivan's and belonged to its age as closely. But Offenbach lacked good librettists, and for this reason you do not stand in long files to buy tickets for Offenbach. You may say that you do not for the more obvious reason that his Operas are never presented in England now-a-days; but the true reason, if you search for it, is that Offenbach never found his Poet, his twin mind. Now Gilbert and Sullivan both lived by the grace of both. Habitually, in actual practice, Gilbert wrote first, plot and lyric, and Sullivan followed; which is the only right order in the making of an Opera, and was convincingly the right order in the making of these men's Operas. For the contribution which Sullivan brought was not only his genius for melody, nor a wit that jumped with Gilbert's, nor a separate and musical wit which revelled in parody. Priceless as these gifts undoubtedly were, above them all (I think) we must reckon the quite marvellous sense of *words* in all his musical settings. You may examine number after number of his, and the more closely you examine the more will you be convinced that no composer ever lived with an exacter appreciation of words, their meaning, their due emphasis, their right articulation. A singer must be a fool indeed if you do not hear through Sullivan's notes the exact language of any song. Take, for example, the well-known Sentry song in *Iolanthe* and attempt to unwed the wit of the air from the wit of the thought and words; or take the Lord Chancellor's song in the same play—

> The law is the true embodiment
> Of everything that's excellent,
> It has no kind of fault or flaw—
> And I, my Lords, embody the law.

and note how Sullivan subdues the air to something almost commonplace and almost silly, but just so as to bring out the intention of demure absurdity, with allowance for every syllable and room for the gesture in the fourth line. Yet should you think he is subduing himself to anything but his artistry, turn to the great duet in *The Sorcerer,* or to the robust Handelian burlesque that winds up "He remains an Englishman" in *H.M.S. Pinafore,* and mark how riotously his own wit takes charge when Gilbert's gives it the rein.

IV

Gilbert had the advantage of setting the themes and dominating the stage-management of the Operas. But before we call his the master-spirit (which by no means implies that it was the more valuable) in the combination, let us take a little evidence from the actors and

singers they commanded. Remind yourselves that these
two men, when they started at the old Opéra Comique,
off the Strand, had to work with the cheapest material.
The "brassiness" of the orchestra during the first run
of *Pinafore*—the combined incompetence in *Patience* of
the vocalists as actors and of the actors as vocalists—
would be incredible today even if faithfully reproduced
to eye and ear. In that first run of *Patience* one or two
of the cast could act a little, one or two could sing a
little; Miss Rosina Brandram alone, asserting that there
would be too much of her in the coming by-and-by,
could do both.

But these two men, combining upon an idea, turned
even shortness of means to their service. They found
themselves in the position long and vainly required by
a neighbour of mine, a great gardener—"I want an
intelligent fellow ready to plant a cabbage upside down
without questioning." Having at first a stage so in-
expensive, a cast which had to listen and obey, they
imposed their idea, or ideas, with a tyranny to which
countless anecdotes bear witness.

The most of these anecdotes are of Gilbert: but
Sullivan, if less irascible in rehearsal, appears to have
been almost as ruthless. Here is the musical procedure,
as related by George Grossmith—who knew it if any
man did:

The music is always learned first. The choruses, finales
etc., are composed first in order; then the quartets, the trios;
the songs last. Sometimes, owing to changes and re-writing,
these are given out to the singers very late (so late that the
singer sometimes found less difficulty in learning the new
tune than in unlearning the old one). The greatest interest
is evinced by all as the new vocal numbers arrive . . .
Sullivan will come suddenly, a batch of MS. under his arm.

and announce that there is something new. He plays over the
new number—the vocal parts only are written. The con-
ductor listens and watches and, after hearing them played
over a few times, contrives to pick up all the harmonies,
casual accompaniments etc. Sullivan is always strict in
wishing that his music shall be sung exactly as he has written
it. One of the leading performers was singing an air at
rehearsal, not exactly dividing the notes as they were written,
giving the general form as it were. "Bravo!" said Sullivan,
"that is really a very good air of yours. Now, if you have
no objection, I will ask you to sing mine."

But the little finger of Gilbert at rehearsal would be
thicker than Sullivan's loins. He kept at home a small
model stage, made to scale, and a box or boxes of tiny
bricks varying in height and colour. These he would
group and re-group in endless patient stage-management
until satisfied just where and just how at any given moment any actor should be standing. Then he would come to
the theatre and, moving everybody about as on a chess-
board, start to bully them into speaking to his exact
wish. To quote Grossmith again:

The music rehearsals are child's play in comparison with
the stage rehearsals. Mr. Gilbert is a perfect autocrat, insisting that his words shall be delivered, even to an inflexion
of the voice, as he dictates. He will stand on the stage and
repeat the words, with appropriate action, over and over
again until they are delivered as he desires.

Add that Gilbert, on top of a detestable temper, had
a tongue like a whip-lash: and—well, you see, as any
of you who wish to be artists must learn in some way,
sooner or later, that there is not only a pleasure in poetic
pains but a tax upon human pains for poetic pleasure.

V

Now, if I have established that Gilbert's is a dominant, even tyrannical brain in these plays which you find so delightful, let us go on to deal with them a little after the manner of Aristotle. Obviously they obey Aristotle in preferring plot to character, even though by inversion: for, his plots being always legal rather than moral in their topsy-turviness (Gilbert, you know, was a barrister and made his first success as a playwright in *Trial by Jury*), his characters behave always on a topsy-turvy legal logic—a logic as mad as Lewis Carroll's or madder; they transfer their affections, or reverse their destinies, by insane rational process—

> Quiet peaceful contemplation
> Disentangles every knot.

A captain in the Royal Navy turns out to have been changed at birth with a common seaman: it follows that, the revelation made, they change places and stations. A promising lad has, by a lapse of terminological exactitude, been apprenticed to a pirate instead of to a pilot; a love-philtre works the wrong way (as it did in *A Midsummer-Night's Dream*); a drummer ascends the throne of Barataria on the affidavit of a foster-mother in eight lines of *recitative*.

Within these limits of absurdity you will notice that all the Operas have limits also in ethic, and are built on an almost rigid convention of design. There is usually an opposition of the Victorian real against the fanciful: of a House of Peers, for example, in robes, against a chorus of fairies under Westminster clock-tower: of a body of Heavy Dragoons against Bunthorne and his lackadaisy maidens. There is almost always a baritone singer, more or less unconnected with the story, introduced with some sort of patter-song—the First Lord's song in *Pinafore* (which, by the way, started its success), the Major-General's in *The Pirates,* the Lord Chancellor's in *Iolanthe,* the Grand Inquisitor's in *The Gondoliers,* and so on. There is also a lady with a contralto voice, who deplores her mature years. The more you examine the Operas to compare them, the closer you will get to a severe and narrow model. And the model in its ethical content is no less straitly laced. It invites you to laugh at the foibles of kings, soldiers, lawyers, artists, and faddists of all sorts. But it touches no universal emotion, no universal instinct even (such as conviviality). Still less does it allow us to think of the base on which Society is built, or admit a thought on it to intrude in any way upon our tom-fooling. We all belong to the upper or upper middle class, or to the class which apes these two. We are all conscious of class distinctions, are a little too consciously snobbish even while we enjoy the exposure of snobbery. The general moral, in fact, is that of the song which he characteristically entitled *King Goodheart:*

> There lived a King, as I've been told,
> In the wonder-working days of old,
> When hearts were twice as good as gold
>   And twenty times as mellow.
> Good temper triumphed in his face,
> And in his heart he found a place
> For all the erring human race
>   And every wretched fellow.
> When he had Rhenish wine to drink
> It made him very sad to think

That some, at junket or at jink,
  Must be content with toddy:
He wished all men as rich as he
(And he was rich as rich could be),
So to the top of every tree
  Promoted everybody. . . .

That King, although no one denies,
His heart was of abnormal size,
Yet he'd have acted otherwise
  If he had been acuter.
The end is easily foretold,
When every blessed thing you hold
Is made of silver, or of gold,
  You long for simple pewter.
When you have nothing else to wear
But cloth of gold and satins rare,
For cloth of gold you cease to care—
  Up goes the price of shoddy:
In short, whoever you may be,
To this conclusion you'll agree,
When every one is somebody,
  Then no one's anybody!

VI

That, you may say, is all very well—or would be well
enough if Gilbert could be cleared as a writer who
genuinely sympathised with some things, or with one
class, and just happened not to sympathise with others.
That is common enough with authors, and especially
with comedians and writers of light verse. Their business being to apply the touch of common sense to human
affairs, one may even allow a certain hardness to be a
part of their outfit [I am ungrateful enough even to find
a certain hardness of surface in that favourite of us all,

C. S. Calverley]. But Gilbert had a baddish streak or two in him; and one in particular which was not only baddish but so thoroughly caddish that no critic can ignore or, in my belief, extenuate it. The man, to summarize, was essentially cruel, and delighted in cruelty. I lay no heavy stress on his addiction—already glanced at—to finding fun in every form of torture and capital punishment. This indeed persists in his work from *The Bab Ballads* right through the plays:

Oh! listen to the tale of little Annie Protheroe;
She kept a small post-office in the neighbourhood of Bow,
She loved a skilled mechanic, who was famous in his day—
A gentle executioner whose name was Gilbert Clay.

I think I hear you say, "A dreadful subject for your
    rhymes!"
O reader, do not shrink—he didn't live in modern times!
He lived so long ago (the sketch will show it at a glance)
That all his actions glitter with the limelight of Romance.

In busy times he laboured at his gentle craft all day—
"No doubt you mean his Cal-craft" you amusingly will say—
But, no—he didn't operate with common bits of string,
He was a Public Headsman, which is quite another thing.

And when his work was over, they would ramble o'er the lea,
And sit beneath the frondage of an elderberry tree;
And ANNIE'S simple prattle entertained him on his walk,
For public executions formed the subject of her talk.

And sometimes he'd explain to her, which charmed her very
    much,
How famous operators vary very much in touch,
And then, perhaps, he'd show how he himself performed the
    trick,
And illustrate his meaning with a poppy and a stick.

It persists (I repeat) through *The Bab Ballads* and into play after play; until, if you are tired and seek a *terminus ad quem,* I suggest this, from *The Mikado,* where an artless maiden sings:

> He shivered and shook as he gave the sign
>   For the stroke he didn't deserve;
> When all of a sudden his eye met mine,
>   And it seemed to brace his nerve.
> For he nodded his head and kissed his hand,
>   And he whistled an air did he,
>   As the sabre true
>   Cut cleanly through
>   His cervical vertebrae!
>   When a man's afraid
>   A beautiful maid
>   Is a charming sight to see.
>   And it's O, I'm glad
>   That moment sad
>   Was soothed by sight of me!

Or—

> To sit in solemn silence, in a dull dark dock,
> In a pestilential prison, with a life-long lock,
> Awaiting the sensation of a short, sharp, shock
> From a cheap and chippy chopper on a big black block.

On this cheap and chippy chopper business I merely observe that Gilbert revelled in it; as anyone else may, so long as I am not asked to join the party.

But Gilbert's cruelty took an uglier twist upon one incurable and unforgivable vice—that of exposing women to public derision on the stage just because they are growing old and losing their beauty. We can forgive Horace or Catullus (if hardly) for venom against

their cast-off mistresses. We should all think the better
of them had they refrained. But the revulsion, even the
vituperation, of a wearied amorist—unpleasant as one
may think it—consists with our experience of men and
women. It is *humanly* vile. What disgusts one in
Gilbert, from the beginning to the end, is his insistence
on the physical odiousness of any woman growing old.
As though, great Heaven! themselves did not find it
tragic enough—the very and necessary tragedy of their
lives! Gilbert shouts it, mocks it, apes with it, spits upon
it. He opens with this dirty trump card in *Trial by
Jury*, where the Judge tells how, as a briefless Barrister:

> I soon got tired of third-class journeys,
>   And dinners of bread and water;
> So I fell in love with a rich attorney's
>   Elderly, ugly daughter.
>
> The rich attorney, he wiped his eyes,
>   And replied to my fond professions:
> "You shall reap the reward of your enterprise,
>   At the Bailey and Middlesex Sessions.
>
> You'll soon get used to her looks," said he,
>   "And a very nice girl you'll find her—
> She may very well pass for forty-three
>   In the dusk, with a light behind her!"

He follows it with "Little Buttercup" in *Pinafore,* in
Patience with

> Fading is the taper waist—
>   Shapeless grows the shapely limb,
> And, although securely laced,
>   Spreading is the figure trim!

> Stouter than I used to be,
>   Still more corpulent grow I—
> There will be too much of me
>   In the coming by-and-by!

—in *The Mikado* with

> The flowers that bloom in the Spring, tra la,
>   Have nothing to do with the case:
> I've got to take under my wing, tra la,
> This most unattractive old thing, tra la,
>   With a caricature of a face.

—and so he proceeds until the end, in *The Mountebanks,* to a scene which almost drove one from the theatre in nausea.

But I dare say the best rebuke of this was the gentle one administered by his favourite actress, Miss Jessie Bond. When she told Gilbert she was going to marry, he burst out, "Little fool!" "I have often," she answered, "heard you say you don't like old women. I shall be one soon. Will you provide for me? You hesitate. Well, I am going to a man who will."

VII

Mr. Rudyard Kipling has observed somewhere that in the life of every happily married man there must come a moment when the sight of his wife at the head of the table suggests the appalling thought that this must go on for ever. Without going so far as this, one may say that even in the happiest marriage one or both of the partners has an occasional sense of some ambition missed. So it happened, we know, in the immensely successful partnership of Gilbert and Sullivan, and it led to frequent quarrels, endeavours on Sullivan's part to break away, finally to estrangement, though happily to no such deadly feud as closed the almost equally successful partnership of MM. Erckmann-Chatrian. Sullivan dreamed that he was capable of High Opera; and so perhaps he was, had he attempted it sooner. But few men can usefully resolve to embrace a new and higher career on their silver wedding-day, and when Sullivan produced *Ivanhoe* at the Royal English Opera House in 1891 it was evident that his resolve had come too late.

But Gilbert, who had bound him to his task, in latter days so sorely against his protestations, also cherished a soaring dramatic ambition. Of men so irascible as he it may usually be observed that they have a bee in their bonnet. (I may use that expression because Gilbert once wore a bonnet as officer in the Gordon Highlanders Militia and had a photograph taken—reproduced in his *Biography*—in the full costume of that gay regiment.) And the very queer bee in Gilbert's bonnet was a violent antipathy against the name and fame of Shakespeare, particularly against the public appreciation of *Hamlet*. It sounds incredible, but there it was. He not only lampooned the great tragedy in a play, *Rosencrantz and Guildenstern:* he never could get away from Hamlet and Ophelia; he had to go on and befool their story, as in *The Mountebanks,* in a silly duet—and again to drag the very weeds and the mud out of Ophelia's end:

> When she found he wouldn't wed her,
> In a river, in a medder,
> Took a header, and a deader
> Was Oph-e-li-a!

Levity, vulgar and blatant!—Yes, and almost we might call it incredible in the man, even if explicable by that same strain of insensitiveness which deadened him to all charity for women past their first youth. It has indeed a like suggestion of impotence.

But insensitiveness will not cover this fault, which actually lay very near the raw. Reading his "Life" and his plays together, we perceive that this neat rhymer, neat wit, neat barrister, neat stage-manager, nursed at the back of his head a conception of himself as a great and serious dramatist—even as Sullivan, with better excuse, nursed the conception of himself as a great composer in Oratorio. Nor did Gilbert fail to realise this conception for want of trying. He has left a number of "serious" dramas behind him—dramas in prose and verse—all more or less unsuccessful on the stage. He even essayed one on the *Faust* theme, fated to allure and defeat all but great souls. He could not see that, whilst genius may be versatile and many-sided, there are certain talents which naturally *exclude* greatness. In his workshop, maybe, he was happy to deem himself possessed of high seriousness. When his efforts came to be produced, the public quite accurately divined that he was not. The discovery cost a not very critical generation of audiences no great effort; but it bit into Gilbert's self-esteem, and he bit upon the wound.

VIII

Most of us in ordinary life have known men who, apt to make fun of others' foibles, show extreme anger or sulkiness when the slightest fun is retorted upon their own. Gilbert was such a man: a professional cynic

W. S. Gilbert 233

and ruthless (as almost all reported anecdotes attest) in wounding with a jest, but extremely touchy—nay, implacably vindictive—when his own withers were wrung, however lightly.

But before he turned to *libretto* Gilbert in his lighter plays, unrewarded by applause, did perhaps as much as his friend Robertson, and more than his friend Byron, to break up by solvent the turgid tradition of mid-Victorian drama and expose its theatricalities. It is usual to ascribe the revolution to Robertson. But Robertson, although he showed a glimmering light towards such reality as exists in "realism," did not—being himself a sentimentalist—probe the real disease of sentimentality. It was Gilbert who probed it and applied the corrosive; and the corrosive proved too strong at first for the public taste: perhaps because it confined itself to destroying the fatty tissue without any promise of healing. At any rate his satirical comedies, deliberately intended to provoke mirth, fell flat; and this no less to their author's bewilderment than to his exasperation.

Let us take *Engaged,* to my mind the best of these, and anyhow characteristic; and let us select one short typical passage. The heroine (or one of them), Miss Treherne, is speaking:

"Cheviot, I have loved you madly, desperately, as other woman never loved other man. *This* poor inexperienced child"—a second heroine—"who clings to me as the ivy clings to the oak, also loves you as woman never loved before. Even, *that* poor cottage maiden, whose rustic heart you so heedlessly enslaved"—a third heroine—"worships you with a devotion which has no parallel in the annals of the heart. In return for all this unalloyed affection, all we ask of you is that you will recommend us to a respectable solicitor."

In those few lines we detect the Gilbertian imbroglio, with the Gilbertian treatment which afterwards served him so well. Yet the public took *Engaged* coldly. To its mind the play wanted a "something."

What? . . . But already we have the answer. Venables anticipated it when he congratulated Thackeray on the success of the *The Four Georges,* delivered as lectures in Willis's Rooms, "Capital, my dear Thack! But you ought to have a piano."

Later on, in Sullivan, Gilbert found his piano, and something more.

But I doubt if, in his own development, he ever progressed an inch deeper in meaning than anything you can find implicit in the passage I have quoted, or (stage-craft apart) any technical skill in lyric or even in plot that he had not anticipated in *The Bab Ballads.* I find—since we talk of pianos—some symbolic truth in the vignette drawn by his own hand and reprinted in successive editions on the title-page of those lays. It represents an infant thumping a piano. You may even read some prophecy in the title of his first real operatic success—*Pinafore.*

IX

At any rate you may assure yourselves, by examination of the *libretti,* that Gilbert, having found his piano, stuck to variations upon a few themes of the *Ballads* and to the end of his career returned to them for his plot. By deft rehandling of their themes, with their originally conceived topsy-turvies and logical reductions to absurdity, he won his success in the partnership; and it is at least some vindication of your elders' intelligence, Gentlemen, that they delighted in this play of mock logic, as they had already fallen to it genially, in their nurseries, over *Alice in Wonderland,* a province of it in which all had been kindly.

For *The Bab Ballads*—if you are wise, you will treat them as wise men treat *Tristram Shandy.* You will not argue, but either like them or leave them alone. I do not compare them as achievements, but simply as they are unsusceptible to criticism; and, however wrong I may be about Gilbert, I have read enough miss-the-mark criticism of Sterne by eminent persons, from Thackeray down, to assert that there are some writings for which criticism has found little guidance between "I Like It" and "I Like It Not."

For my part I rejoice in *The Bab Ballads,* and find them on the whole considerably superior to the lyrics with which Gilbert diversified the Operas. Nor can I easily believe that, being the man he was, he deliberately and artistically keyed down his wit to the requirements of the music and of stage-presentation. He may have done so half consciously. The possibility, however, suggests a question on which we may conclude.

X

An examination of Gilbert's and Sullivan's success in sometimes wedding, sometimes alternating, words with music to produce a genuine, if narrow, form of Light Opera may be of some use to those who accept, as to those who on its results feel a little doubtful about accepting, the Wagnerian and post-Wagnerian claims for Grand Opera. I feel some timidity in advancing so much as a foot over this ground; since of all hierophants those of music are the most scornful of intruders who would ally their pet art with others that make life enjoyable. I observe also that the majority of these apostles of harmony are as intense in vendetta as incapable of explaining what it is all about; so that one wavers in amaze between the "interpretations" in the programme of any Symphony Concert and the Billingsgate in which these critics pursue their sacerdotal loves and hates.

But I suppose that, after all, it works out to this:

(1) Grand Opera, like any other opera, is an artificial thing; a lovely form of art if its components of drama, words and music be intelligently blended, yet always so artificial that the audience's imagination and intelligence must be invited together to assist in their own captivation.

(2) If these three elements (to omit scenery) of drama, words and music could be captured, each at its highest, *and perfectly blended,* we should have perfection in one combined form of art.

(3) But this combination implies that each contributory has its due place, each giving its best and yet subduing it to the others' best, at the right moment: that suppose, for example, one could enlist Shakespeare and Beethoven together for an Opera of *Lear,* or Molière and Mozart for a *Don Giovanni,* still the composing authors must each submit his genius to the total result.

(4) Now the trouble is that such things don't happen in this world.

(5) But suppose the theory sound. Of all men of genius Wagner was perhaps the worst equipped with those concomitants which his theory demanded. Therefore, being one of the most arrogant of men, he put music in supreme command and tortured our divinest of gifts—the modulated speaking voice for which Sophocles and Shakespeare wrote—to speak *through* music; which is to say, largely *against* it. It is not for

me to do more than marvel at the genius for orchestration which stunned or mesmerized sensible men into accepting a megalomaniac theory which, coolly examined, bears about as much identity with any notions of the great masters of poetry, painting, music, as did the dismembered carcasses before the tent of awaking crapulous Ajax with the tall captains from whose imagined slaughter he had reeled to bed. The temperate voice of the eighteenth century may whisper something salutary at this point: for, after all, Joshua Reynolds *could* paint.

I believe—says Reynolds—it may be considered as a general rule, that no art can be grafted with success on another art. For although they all profess the same origin, and to proceed from the same stock, yet each has its own peculiar mode of imitating nature and of deviating from it, each for the accomplishment of its own particular purpose. These deviations, more especially, will not bear transplantation to another soil.

Now Reynolds may easily be wrong if we apply this observation to opera in general, as presumably Hazlitt would have applied it. "The opera," says Hazlitt, "is the most artificial of all things . . . it is an illusion and a mockery. . . . A headache may be produced by a profusion of sweet smells or sweet sounds; but we do not like the headache the more on that account. Nor are we reconciled to it, even at the opera."

But the Attic Theatre proved, centuries ago, that speech and music, with dancing and scenery, could be brought together to produce one of the very highest forms of art, *provided that each of the contributories were kept in its proper place.* Aristotle recognised this, of course; and, to use our immediate subject for an illustration, Gilbert and Sullivan prove that the difficulty of bringing together accomplished pedestrian speech and accomplished music can be solved *ambulando,* if the rule of keeping them in their proper places be observed more or less as the Greeks observed it. As I have said, a combination of supreme poetry with supreme music and a variety of the other arts at their very best is not granted by the gods to the generations of men; but it seems evident that in some happy moments the co-operation of poet and musician, neither of the first eminence, may almost chemically produce a new thing which, if not transcendent, is extremely pleasing, at once novel and reasonably permanent in its appeal. Opera is an artificial thing. It is not made less artificial on a theory of "realism" which disguises nature under a new artificiality such as the *leit-motif,* this *leit-motif* being actually as much of a convention as the labels enclosing words which primitive painters and caricaturists drew as issuing from the mouths of their figures. It is, I suggest, greatly to Sullivan's credit that with his in-comparable talent for articulating speech in music, he resisted all temptation of that talent to obscure or deafen by music the spoken words which must be the back-bone of all drama since they carry and advance the plot.

And—for a last word—it may even be that your delight in Gilbert and Sullivan testifies to a natural un-conscious revolt against the theory of opera so prevalent in our time. We know from the history of the Theatre —from the tyranny, for example, laid upon it so long by the theories of Castelvetro and his followers—that a barbarous mistake can be ferociously enforced by pedantry. Against such pedantry a childlike instinct may sometimes usefully assert itself, insisting "But the Emperor *has* no clothes!"

ADDRESSES

OPENING OF KEATS HOUSE, HAMPSTEAD
THE MEMORY OF SIR WALTER SCOTT

OPENING OF KEATS HOUSE
HAMPSTEAD

May 9th, 1925

Mr. Mayor, Ladies and Gentlemen,

I

Because this occasion is, for "a little clan," a monumental one: and because the memory of Keats seems to me in some danger of being over-laboured just now: I shall try to recall you to some of those simplicities which always best become a simple monument.

But first let me congratulate you, Mr. Mayor, upon the occasion—

> There may be cities that refuse
> To their own child his honours due.

But Hampstead is not one of these. Always in Hampstead, going by its walks or on the edge of its heath, any man of letters must be haunted by thoughts which seem to him almost memories: of a great literary tradition merging still—please Heaven!—into a great literary future. Still of the town, yet not of the town —but fragrant, on the country's rim—these ghosts, thoughts, memories, accompany or tread close on the musing mind. A statue or an obelisk were an offence

to the *genius loci;* which pursues rather along the shade
of a paling or under a tree that in a time before ours
once

in a drear-nighted December

showed a part of its frosted branches to the lamp-light,
or in spring budded to arrest a poet's step on your path-
ways or broke into leaf and held, on this verge over
London, an immortal nightingale captive.

II

And so, Sir, it is surely to Hampstead's credit, that
you have chosen, instead of an obelisk or statue, to
preserve this simple house in perpetuity for a memorial
of *John Keats.*   In this house he agonised with love and
despondency: on a bed in a chamber above us he read
in a drop of blood his death warrant: from the door
beyond that passage he departed on his last journey—
brave and hopeless as Henry Fielding on *his* last voyage.
In the dim garden outside yonder pane of glass he
heard the Hampstead nightingale and translated that
song "not born for death" into human speech as near
to heavenly as any we can dare to snatch out of this
transitory life to call immortal. . . .   Still on the edge
and shadow of that trench untimely digged we invoke
that genius, fleet as water, "writ in water."

Still are thy pleasant voices, thy nightingales awake:
For Death he taketh all away: but them he cannot take!

"Men are we and must mourn." *Mentem mortalia
tangunt.*   But here, Sir, in this room—in this house—
you preserve almost all that a decent, necessary piety can
preserve.

III

Let me say frankly that your guest, whom you over-compliment by standing him here, could do very well without any memorials beyond the poems themselves—beyond the great Odes (say) some Sonnets, *La Belle Dame sans Merci, The Eve of St. Agnes, Hyperion* and lines of *Endymion* chanted in the ear of his own youth. These and such things are to me the pure, the mere, the miraculous, the only considerable Keats.

I assert this in face of a most formidable company, far more learned than I: and I assert it in this haunted house. Through its chambers walks—and now must walk—the shade of Fanny Brawne, by the favour of whose grand-daughter, present to-night, many mementoes have been bestowed as its treasure. I shall say but a word of Fanny Brawne. She was young, sprightly (as she had, by virtue of her graces, a right to be), and as Touchstone said to Jaques

> if ladies be but young and fair,
> They have the gift to know it.

That Keats tortured himself over his passion for her is, of course, evident from his published letters. But one guesses that he would, in his febrile breaking health, have tortured himself almost equally in any passionate flame. She was not (if you will) the woman for him. But ask yourselves, of your experience of life, Who could have been? The few words she discreetly left of him in her later married life are sensible and most tender. Let us leave it at that. I wish, for my part, that the letters had never been exhumed. But they were: and they do *her* no harm.

IV

For we know—do we not?—that to any actual Keats any Fanny Brawne can never be the woman *we* criticise as sprightly or worldly or of breeding and self-possession, but is always an ideal creation in a lover's brain. Oh, believe me, Ladies and Gentlemen, you can as soon explain a play of Shakespeare's by imagining him in search along his shelves for his next plot, as you can explain Keats by Fanny Brawne, Fanny Brawne by Keats, or Dulcinea del Toboso by any process but that of Don Quixote's brain. There is a little of the poet in every man here: and if we did not all, rough men, poetise somewhat our selected mates, I ask you, How could the world go on? Who, above all, is to select mates for poets? What expert? What official? No, they must do it for themselves, and unhappily when they don't at first succeed they too often try, try again.

V

Edward FitzGerald, to my thinking the best critic of his Victorian contemporaries, took up the love-letters of Keats straight after a study of Catullus: and (wrote he) to James Russell Lowell—But let me pause upon that name to regret that Miss Amy Lowell, whose two erudite massive volumes on Keats almost make me afraid to speak, weighing "as an ox on my tongue," cannot be here to-night as she intended. Let us all wish her a happy and speedy recovery!

To resume—Edward FitzGerald wrote (February 18, 1878):

When Keats came, I scarce felt a change from Catullus, both such fiery Souls as wore out their Bodies early; and I

can even imagine Keats writing such filthy Libels against any
one he had a spite against, even Armitage Brown, had Keats
lived 2,000 years ago.

Yes, and for two other reasons I connect always in
my mind these two Thalia's sons—Keats with Catullus:
these two who died in their prime, died at apparently
such spendthrift irreparable waste of the gods' promise;
died early because forsooth the gods loved them. For
the first reason (which may seem trivial, but is not
when searched) both passionately loved their family,
their brothers. Catullus' *Frater ave atque vale* has come
sighing to us down the ages, to be taken up and continued by Keats' devotional tears and lament over "poor
Tom": and who can forget that picture of little John
Keats, aged seven or thereabouts, posting himself sentry
in his night-shirt with a sword outside his mother's
sick-room—that picture which FitzGerald so often and
urgently begged Millais to paint?

VI

But records of children and brothers wildly devoted
are common enough, you will say. Well then, for my
second point of likeness, I say that of these two poets,
when all the dross of their work has been sifted out, the
residue is absolute gold, pure and proof against whatever touchstone brought. And therefore can anyone
name two stars in literature over whom we more wonder
at—even though we upbraid not—the gods for slaying
their darlings young, over whose twin trench we stretch
more yearning impotent hands? Says Robert Bridges:

If one English poet might be recalled to-day from the dead
to continue the work which he left unfinished on earth, it is

probable that the crown of his country's desire would be set on the head of John Keats.

An idle regret, on an idle speculation! True: as all regrets, all speculations, wander around the foreknowing path of the gods—as Keats himself, for example, wanders in the maze of *Endymion.*

VII

An idle speculation! It might have been that, relieved of personal disease and selfish torment (a part of it), Keats had opened the door wider on that larger vision revealed in *Hyperion.*

> "High Prophetess," said I, "purge off
> Benign, if so it please thee, my mind's film"—
> "None can usurp this height," return'd that Shade,
> "But those to whom the miseries of the world
> *Are* miseries, and will not let them rest."

As idle the regret!

There are no voices, O Rhodope! that are not soon mute, however tuneful: there is no name, with whatever emphasis of passionate love repeated, of which the echo is not faint at last.

Catullus is dead: Keats is dead: and the ghost of the girl he idealised has gone out, somewhere, to dance and wear away, if she can, "the everlasting flint." But here is the house inhabited, out yonder the tree, the garden, the listener to that song not born for death while poetry lasts.

VIII

I have personal reason to know, Sir, the domesticity which guards and respects, for the mere sake, even quite modest literature in Hampstead. I have real reason to know how far from this clearer height over London even a faint invalid voice can travel for the good of an uncounted many. Hampstead is not a parade-ground of authors, nor a Campo Santo for tall monuments. It is and has been, in a gentle pre-eminence and dignity, a *home* of genius. I like, Sir, to think it our way to celebrate even our most illustrious poets in this modest, homely fashion: that as, a few days ago, Englishmen gathered in a country churchyard to honour Gray, so we to-night have gathered to this house of Keats as a shrine in your City.

THE MEMORY OF
SIR WALTER SCOTT [1]

My Lord Provost, My Lords, Ladies and Gentlemen,

I

You have cast far for a President this year, though you might of course have found many nearer and more eminent—better able certainly to acknowledge the honour which, at this moment, naturally oppresses the heart and tongue. But you could not (and this must be my justification), though you flung your net in waters far remoter than the caves of Cornwall where lies my home, have dragged up a more inveterate (shall I say a more crustacean?) lover of that great man whose memory an admitted Southron must presently, by the privilege of invitation, invite you to honour.

II

You know by report that I lecture at Cambridge and there have sometimes to lecture upon Shakespeare. *That* is a career to which, as few Professors can escape it, some evolutionary instinct of self-protection has taught us to adapt ourselves.

But sometimes, dealing with Shakespeare, I have

[1] Speech at the Twenty-seventh Annual Dinner of The Edinburgh Sir Walter Scott Club, Nov. 26, 1926.

harked back upon Scott; and have pondered upon the different ways which History has chosen to assign her record of the two greatest imaginative writers in our literature.

To Shakespeare, she has left "a local habitation and a name." What else? Truly we know nothing apart from a very few constated facts and a vast deal of trumpery gossip.

But of Scott, that other inspired charmer of souls, we know far more (probably) than has ever been recorded of any writer in history. Apart from his own illustrious Prefaces and Notes and Appendixes, we have not only the monumental *Life* by his Son-in-law Lockhart— perhaps next to Boswell's Johnson, the finest biography in our language (you Scots hold the palm in Biography anyway), but Letters and Journals etc., line upon line, revelation upon familiar revelation of the actual man.

III

And there is the difference. Theoretically would you really wish—ought any of us really to wish—to know more of Shakespeare than we do? I ask, would you confidently wish it? I know this is a bold question. But I would ask you the like of Homer. Do we really want more for our image of Homer than the words of the Hymn attributed to him?—"Farewell, O maidens of Delos, and hereafter if any stranger landing on your beach should enquire 'Who was the sweetest singer ever sung to you?' make answer to him modestly—'Sir, he was just a blind man and came (he said) from rocky Chios.'" All the "Lives" of Shakespeare when the pot is skimmed boil down to this—that there was a boy in Stratford who left it to try his fortune with the London theatre-people, learned to write superbly but still hankered after his native banks of Avon, and ended as a neighbour respected by his neighbours—a man not forgetting his roots. As Bagehot remarks in effect, of the passage in *Venus and Adonis* describing the tremors of a hare aroused at sound of his pursuers, "Who says, after this, that we know nothing of Shakespeare? We know that he had once been after a hare."

Now what I come to, My Lord Provost, is this, that of Scott—apart from the operation of genius, which is always a mystery—we are left with no mystery at all, and we want none.

We know that this Wizard of the North wore no Prospero's mantle, that he drew no cabalistic circle save that of the writing-lamp under which his figures—Di' Vernon or Jeanie Deans, Marmion, or Richard of England, Edie Ochiltree or Dugald Dalgetty—weave their dance at his call. We know that he, too, had been after a hare: after salmon too, and the running deer. But we see this man, alike in his poems and novels and in his own life so amply recorded, as almost the sincerest figure of a great Scots gentleman—"the Shirra"—*totus teres:* a figure so vivid, so sincere and simple, that only certain great simple characters in fiction—Don Quixote, My Uncle Toby, The Vicar of Wakefield, Mr. Pickwick —occupy in our affection a place comparable with this actual man, who rode Ettrick and survives to us, himself as romantic as any of the characters he created.

IV

A month or two since, Sir—your Club's invitation giving me excuse to satisfy an old craving, one of those which conceived in boyhood are so often deferred

to the lazier daily task which nevertheless must be done
—I made pious pilgrimage through a good part of the
Border. The weather was perfect, the sky clear blue
above those enfolding hills; the hillsides were sheeted
down in such green enchantment as ever ringed Thomas
the Rymer beneath Eildon Tree. And I tell you, Sir,
that at every lap of the hills under circuitous Tweed
I could see the Shirra riding down on his grey pony—
a figure held somehow in the imagination of one's boyhood, inseparable even then between adoration of his
writings and love of their author. On a return from
some of these pilgrimages there followed a Sunday night
of thunderstorm, memorable (I was told) even in these
parts, and next day, visiting Lasswade for the site of his
early farm-steading, I learned what Esk could do in
spate, and knew again this younger man with his lame
leg pressed to the saddle-flap daring (as Lockhart tells)
the fords.

V

They tell us now-a-days that Romance is dead and
Scott neglected. Romance is never dead. As our greatest living Romantic puts it, Romance brings up the 9.15;
and she always will. But there has been some neglect
of Scott among Lecturers and School Masters, who
still talk indefatigably of the Romantic Movement or
a Romantic Revival, of which he and Byron were the
tallest Champions. Some while ago your new President,
Professor Grierson, gave us a most vivifying lecture on
the word "Romantic" and I had shamefacedly to confess,
when thanking him for it afterwards, I did quite recently
advise my pupils that for a time we should give the
words "Romantic" and "Classical" a rest. Of course

I was wrong. We can never give even the word "Romantic" a rest; but I was thinking of an admired Lecturer who came to Cambridge and advertised a series of Lectures on the Romantic Revival. Some of my pupils came to me to read some of the poetry of the early 19th century, and when I asked what passages of Byron had been recommended to them they admitted that Byron had not been included in the Syllabus. I forget if Scott was. But Byron!—"God shield us, a lion among ladies!"

Nay, I regret to say that, but yesterday, I had read to me a Chapter of my old friend Sir Walter Raleigh *On Writing and Writers*—the Chapter was entitled *On the Decline and Fall of Romanticism in 19th Century Poetry*. Now as they used to say at Oxford "Raleigh was a Prince"; he was at any rate a man of his hands; above all Professors the man who despised lecturing, as he put it, "for the School Ma'am"; and although he had much to say for the impetus which made the Romantic Movement, I sought in vain for the name of Scott. Burns was mentioned. Many years ago I found myself in very hot water through asking innocently in a weekly paper why Scotsmen spent a disproportionate amount of enthusiasm on Burns as compared with Scott. I shall not revive that controversy to-night, for fear of physical violence, save to say that had I the honour to be one of Scott's countrymen I would beat the racial tom tom in his honour above all other men of your jealous race.

But, Sir, I remember here, that I am a Professor, and as such, perhaps, have my only justification for the honour of addressing you—if I can find it.

Well, to begin with, I do not see how any professorial talk consorts with an occasion like this, at so many of which Scott himself assisted and (according to Hogg) could outtoast all compotators, for the final toast standing with one leg on his chair, the other (lame) on the table, after what I understand to have been a laudable national custom.   It still is, maybe; but I hope to be excused presently from *that* challenge.[1]

VI

But of Scott as a writer let me just say three words and those very briefly :—

In the first place few men, I think, unless or until their business obliges them to follow some way into English (I hardly dare add Scottish) literature, can realise how much this man had read, digested and known; in a word what a scholar he was, how careless in grace, yet how profound.   I can only bring my own tribute of testimony to this, for what it is worth.   But it happens that for some years I have been working on the comedies of Shakespeare, and always I am finding, in stray footnote or recollection or hint, that Scott some-how, somewhere, has been there before.   It is not, as it is with Johnson, always a definite pronouncement of Common-sense.   I should compare it rather with Dante's search for a literary language among the Italian dialects of his time.   Always ahead of us, as Dante says, is "the panther of our quest"; in no province his abiding lair.   So, in early literature, nowhere is Scott's abiding lair, yet always Scott has been that way—always in reading Scott, in almost any dozen pages, say of the *Talisman* or of *Nigel,* we are haunted by undertones, overtones of Shakespeare: so, reading Shakespeare, you catch, borne back out of somewhere on a whisper, the horn of elfland blowing, the music of the leading hound—

---

[1] The speaker was himself temporarily a cripple, through an accident.

Long I follow'd happy guides,
I could never reach their sides;
Their step is forth and, ere the day
Breaks, up their leaguer and away. . . .
On eastern hills I see their smokes
Mix'd with mist by distant lochs.

So it is with anyone who has once surrendered his mind to these two, our most imaginative writers.

VII

He had, we know, an incomparable gift of verbal memory: comparable only in the next generation with that of your other countryman, Macaulay. All records attest it, even if we discount those of that egregious Shepherd (if in this company I may call him so) whose effigy today sits, as somebody ordained it to be, on a brae over sweet St. Mary's Loch, irremoveable as the Shepherd himself was when for the best part of two days and nights he sat attendant upon the conversation of Scott and John Murray, the publisher. But this gift of memorising, while a respectable mystery to me, can be shared by any "Calculating Boy." The real mystery to me, Sir, is the *understanding* that went with it, and communicated itself all over Europe.

Here was a man, intensely and actively conservative: a hater of the French Revolution and all it meant: a close clannish Scot, moreover—to whom his family ties and Tweed were Jordan and meant more than any Abana or Pharpar, rivers of Damascus. And yet from the circle of his writing-lamp radiated a something that made all European literature different. Even as, from a little monastery in Jarrow, Bede's candle cast its beam across fen marsh and channel fog to the Continent and

Charlemagne's court, so the Waverley novels reached our dear enemy France and (more than ever Byron did, the more admired) rekindled romance over Europe. That is my second wonder—who talk to you as a man of letters: and I must leave it at that.

But let me fetch back the recollections from the far away 90's to which I suppose I must date myself. In those days our dear enemy France was getting back, as they say, something of her own, by opposing new Realism to the Old Romance and uniting it with the anxious cultivation of style, the search for the exact word—*le mot juste*. Flaubert and de Maupassant were models in those days; with Tourguénieff, who was a Russian, but spent his life in exile in Paris. We sought back to Balzac and Stendhal too. But a man there was, to rescue us from the Desert of Realism—one gallant Scotsman, the adored of us all, hopeless beyond our imitation, who kept the flag of Scott flying and carried it till he fell. I mean of course Robert Louis Stevenson.

My Lord Provost, while Scotland stands where it did it is impossible that Romance should die: this very gathering to-night testifies that it yet fervently lives.

VIII

For my third and last point of remark, I must (how shall I put it?) hitch up an old shooting-jacket between two wizard robes—that of the younger Scott, the poet, and the mature Scott of the novels (prolific, strong, then wearied, broken, but yet carrying through with honour, to the end). And I find, or try to find, some reconciliation of the two literary Walter Scotts in *this*—

All readers of all records, letters, anecdotes, must wonder, in these times, at the boisterous animal spirits of the man. He had always a fund of them—let me put it—more than sufficient for his immediate purposes, or for those of his friends over whose misadventures in his company he would laugh till the tears ran down his cheeks, whether he or they took a toss off horseback into a bog, or were sunk in a coracle at salmon-spearing and must swim for it in the perilous dark. So he would have rocked with laughter at the spectacle of a man pursuing his hat down the Canongate. There is a Homeric simplicity in all Scott's laughter; and to that same Homeric simplicity we owe and, criticising, yet bless the rush and spate of his verse in *The Lay,* and in *Marmion.* Monckton Milnes, Lord Houghton, doubted in verse if our forefathers were really finer fellows than the best of later years: but he noted in verse one gallant difference :—

> To them was life a simple art
>   Of duties to be done,
> A game where each man took his part,
>   A race where all must run;
> A battle whose great scheme and scope
>   They little cared to know,
> Content as men-at-arms to cope
>   Each with his fronting foe.
>
> Man now his Virtue's diadem
>   Puts on and proudly bears:
> Great thoughts, great feelings came to *them*
>   Like instincts, unawares.
> Blending their soul's sublimest needs
>   With tasks of every day,
> They went about their gravest deeds
>   As noble boys at play.

And I suggest to you that this same store of Homeric (or if you prefer it) of Sabine vigour carried Scott through. It is nonsense to say that in the novels he is no artist. Beginning with a wayward loose rein in *Waverley,* he runs loose again in *Guy Mannering,* and then, in *The Antiquary,* finds himself. Who will say that *The Antiquary* is not great constructive art? Or that *Old Mortality, The Heart of Midlothian, Redgauntlet* are not master-works? Those prosperous happy years, by Lockhart with how delicate a familiarity described! Thenafter the tale of ruin, of "all lost save honour" and still of honour winning through. I shall not touch on this, Sir, save to suggest that even the bravest knight, not carried through on the almost spent tide of Scott's amazing vitality, must have gone down under the waves.

IX

At the very close almost—broken and near spent—he came to his native City, to make his will. A spell of most violent weather immured him, and his good friend Mr. Cadell persuaded him to remove to the hospitable house in Atholl Crescent, where for several days he wrote manfully at *Count Robert of Paris.* There, pestered by his publisher Ballantyne for an omitted motto, he moved to the window, gazed out on the whirl of the storm, and invented the few lines, subscribed *The Deluge,* that form the motto of Chapter v.

> The storm increases; 'tis no sunny shower
> Fostered in the moist breath of March or April,
> Or such as parchèd Summer cools his lips with.
> Heaven's windows are flung wide; the inmost deeps

Call in hoarse greeting one upon another;
On comes the flood in all its foaming horrors,
And where's the dike shall stop it?

My Lord Provost, I have seen (I say) and could not help seeing the solid vision of this full-blooded high-mettled man riding down to dangerous fords by Tweed and Esk and Yarrow: I have heard the ripple of his river under Abbotsford and walked back up the meadow to assure myself that what Lockhart tells is not fable: it may well have been the last quiet music lulling him. But here, in the story I have quoted, is Mr. Valiant-for-Truth riding down to the last wildest ford of all, always the great man, bequeathing his sword to any that can deserve it, his great bow to any that can bend it.

And I say—speaking from my heart, and from my knowledge, such as it is—that no writer of this Island has left at once so much of his genius abiding in the world for its clean delight, so much invention to entrance so many young and old, so gallant and good an example of good living, as has this exemplar of a great Scottish gentleman—whose most noble memory I now ask you, Mesdames and Sirs, rising to pledge.

My Lord Provost, my Lords, Ladies and Gentlemen, I lift my glass with you to the well-beloved memory of Walter Scott.

INDEX

Addison, Joseph, 7
Allingham, William, 211
Ariosto, 107
Aristophanes, 110, 111
Aristotle, 108, 113, 178
Arnold, Matthew, 20, 49, 143, 205
Austen, Jane, 77

Bacon, Francis, 213
Barnes, William, 50, 138
Basse, William, 29
Baudelaire, Charles, 49
Beaumont, Francis, 7, 113
Bede, 254
Beerbohm, Max, 148
Bennett, Arnold, 209
Blake, William, 98
Boccaccio, 107
Bond, Jessie, 230
Boswell, James, 56, 249
Brandram, Rosina, 222
Brawne, Fanny, 243 ff.
Bridges, Robert, 3, 50
Brougham, Lord, 152
Brown, T. E., 50
Browne, Sir Thomas, 10, 193
Browne, William, 29
Browning, Elizabeth Barrett, 5
Browning, Robert, 140, 141, 206
Bunyan, John, 56
Burke, Edmund, 148 ff.
Burns, Robert, 18, 48, 98, 99, 252
Bury, Richard de, 215
Byron, George Gordon, Lord, 48, 57, 251, 252

Calderon, 108
Calverley, C. S., 227
Carlyle, Thomas, 191
Cartwright, William, 32
Castelvetro, 104, 108
Catullus, 228, 245
Cervantes, 108
Chambers, Sir Edmund, 19, 25

Champneys, Basil, 129, 137, 138, 141, 142
Chaucer, Geoffrey, 27, 107, 192, 195
Coleridge, Samuel Taylor, 58 ff.
Cory (Johnson), William, 10
Courtney of Penwith, Lord, 206
Cowley, Abraham, 13, 14, 15, 16, 28
Cowper, William, 48
Crashaw, Richard, 33
Crewe, Lord Chief Justice, 187
Croce, Benedetto, 180

Dante, 5, 190, 253
Dark, Sidney, 182
Darwin, Erasmus, 99
Davidson, John, 113
Dekker, Thomas, 104
De Quincey, Thomas, 90
de Sélincourt, Prof. E., 77
Dickens, Charles, 55
Donne, John, 31, 32, 202
Drummond, William, of Hawthornden, 28
Dryden, John, 33, 148–9
Duclaux, Madame, 170

Elton, Oliver, 170
Emerson, Ralph Waldo, 106

Fielding, Henry, 242
FitzGerald, Edward, 244
Fletcher, John, 113
Fletcher, Phineas, 29
Forster, John, 55
Frazer, Sir James, 20
Froude, James Anthony, 56

Garnett, Richard, 143
Gaskell, Elizabeth, 56
Gay, John, 39
"George Eliot," 70
Gibbon, Edward, 145, 146

259

Index

Gilbert, Sir William Schwenk, 216 ff.
Godley, A. D., 174
Goldsmith, Oliver, 14, 44, 208
Gower, John, 195
Gray, Thomas, 7, 44 ff., 247
Grey, of Fallodon, 84
Grossmith, George, 222

Hadrian, 52
Hallam, Arthur Henry, 11
Hardy, Thomas, 54
Harvey, Gabriel, 26, 196
Hazlitt, William, 61, 91, 126
Herbert, George, 114
Herrick, Robert, 29
Hervey, William, 13, 15
Heywood, Thomas, 104
Hogg, James, 252, 254
Homer, 192, 249
Horace, 228
Houghton, Lord (Monckton Milnes), 127, 256
Hunt, Leigh, 124

Irving, Washington, 7

Jackson, Henry, 199
Jefferies, Richard, 166
Jeffery, Dr. John, 193
Jeffrey, Francis, Lord, 63
Johnson, Samuel, 3 ff., 98, 253
Jones, Inigo, 116
Jonson, Ben, 27, 104

Keats, John, 29, 241 ff.
Ker, W. P., 170
King, Edward, 10, 11, 12
King, Henry (Bishop), 34
Kipling, Rudyard, 230

Labiche, 111
Lamb, Charles, 37, 91
Landor, Walter Savage, 11
Lang, Matheson, 207
"Lewis Carroll," 235
Lincoln, Abraham, 184
Livingstone, R. W., 190 n.
Lockhart, John Gibson, 249
Longfellow, Henry Wadsworth, 204, 205
Longinus, 143 ff.
Lope de Vega, 108
Lowell, Amy, 244
Lyly, John, 113

Macaulay, Lord, 205-6, 254
Maclean, Catherine, 77, 78
Mandeville, Sir John, 107
Mantuan, 53
"Mark Rutherford," 56
Marot, 53
Marvell, Andrew, 18
Masson, David, 11
Menander, 110, 111
Meredith, George, 79, 110, 111, 127, 161
Meynell, Alice, 8
Mill, John Stuart, 143
Milton, John, 4 ff., 190, 196
Molière, 108, 110, 111
Montaigne, Miguel de, 160
More, Sir Thomas, 195
Morley, Edith J., 88
Morley, Henry, 133
Moschus, 21
Moses, 157

Newman, John Henry (Cardinal), 180
Noel, Roden, 50
North, Christopher, 64

Offenbach, 220
Osborn, E. B., 189-90

Pater, Walter, 40
Patmore, Coventry, 106, 122 ff.
Payne, E. J., 153
Philips, Ambrose, 38
Plato, 58, 76, 147-8, 190
Poe, Edgar Allan, 205
Pope, Alexander, 29
Prior, Matthew, 39 ff.

Quarterly Review, 6, 208

Raleigh, Sir Walter, Professor, 104, 252
Reynolds, Sir Joshua, 14, 237
Roberts, W. Rhys, 143 ff.
Robinson, Henry Crabb, 88
Robortello, Francis, 145
Rossetti, Dante Gabriel, 22
Ruskin, John, 128

Saintsbury, George, 169, 213
Sappho, 156
Sargent, John, 140
Scott, Sir Walter, 248 ff.

Shakespeare, William, 8, 17, 32, 57, 101 ff., 190, 248, 249, 250
Shelley, Percy Bysshe, 33, 48, 59–61
Sidgwick, Henry, 165 ff., 214
Simonides, 17
Smith, Rt. Hon. W. H., 219
Spencer, Herbert, 151
Spenser, Edmund, 22 ff.
Sterne, Laurence, 235
Stevenson, Robert Louis, 255
Sullivan, Sir Arthur, 216 ff.
Surrey, Earl of, 195
Swinburne, Algernon Charles, 49

Tennyson, Lord, 11, 49, 50, 125, 137, 140, 141
Thackeray, William Makepeace, 55, 234
Theocritus, 18 ff.
Thompson, Francis, 71

Thomson, James, 99, 146
Tyrwhitt, Thomas, 119

Vaughan, Henry, 35
Virgil, 21 ff.
Voltaire, 190

Wagner, 235
Walpole, Horace, 220
Wellington, Duke of, 183, 184
Welsted, Leonard, 143
Wilson, Prof. J. Dover, 197 n.
Wither, George, 36 ff.
Wordsworth, Christopher (Bishop), 84
Wordsworth, Dorothy, 54 ff.
Wordsworth, Mary, 63 ff.
Wordsworth, William, 48, 58 ff.
Wright, William Aldis, 118
Wyat, Sir Thomas, 195
Wycherley, William, 33